Catal Hüyük

Turkey, c. 7200-5800 BC

Archaeologists believe that Catal Hüyük, in southern Turkey, may have been the world's first city, built over 9,000 years ago. So far its ruins have revealed only some of their secrets.

About forty years ago, archaeologists began to excavate a mound in a remote part of southern Turkey. Their fascinating discoveries changed what we know about the earliest civilizations.

As they worked, the team exposed the ruins of an ancient city older than any that had been found anywhere in the world. They called it Catal Hüyük.

Catal Hüyük dates back to about 7200 BC – over 9,000 years ago. At least 6,000 people lived there. Among them were skilled craftsmen – builders, weavers, potters, and others.

City of mysteries

The people of Catal Hüyük had no written language, so they left behind no account of how they lived.

Archaeologists have had to piece together the story of their lives by sifting through what is left of the city. But there are still many unsolved mysteries about Catal Hüyük. Why was it built in such a remote spot? Why did the houses have their doors on the roofs? Why are so many of the buildings decorated with plaster models of bulls' heads? Who lived in Catal Hüyük, and what were their daily lives like?

Hunting country

Catal Hüyük was built on the site of a dried-up lake where the soil was good for growing crops. There were forests in the mountains about 50 miles (80 kilometers) away, so there was a plentiful supply of timber for building. Nearby there was good hunting country where gazelles and wild asses roamed – but there were also lions, leopards, and bears, so hunting could be dangerous.

In many ways, the buildings of Catal Hüyük were like those in other ancient cities. They were made of mud bricks held together with a wooden framework.

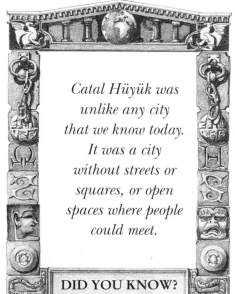

Catal Hüyük was unlike any city that we know today. It was a city without streets or squares, or open spaces where people could meet.

DID YOU KNOW?

This reconstruction of a shrine room at Catal Hüyük shows how richly decorated the shrines were, with real bulls' horns mounted in plaster heads and paintings of vultures on the walls. Offerings of precious objects are being made while a burial takes place.

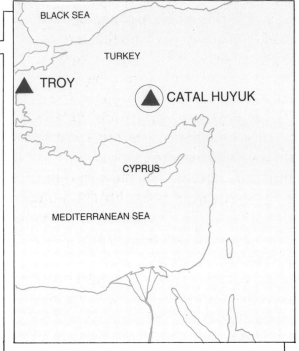

The remains of Catal Hüyük are in southern Turkey. They are about 31 miles (50 kilometers) south of Konya and 200 miles (320 kilometers) south of Ankara, the capital city of Turkey.

They had flat roofs, with plaster gutters to carry away rain water. But what made Catal Hüyük so different from other cities was that the houses had no doors at ground level. People went in and out through a trapdoor or through a door in a kind of hallway built on the roof.

The streetless city

Even stranger, people moved about the city by walking across the roofs. The houses were joined together, with no streets and few open spaces. Where buildings were different heights, they were connected by wooden ladders.

One advantage of having no doors at ground level was that the city needed no wall to protect its inhabitants from wild animals or human enemies. If they took away the ladders linking their homes, they were quite safe.

If this was the idea, it seems to have worked. Unlike most other ancient cities, Catal Hüyük does not appear to have been attacked or conquered.

Living on the roof

The houses of Catal Hüyük were small and must have been rather cramped, although in fine weather families could use their flat roofs as extra living space. Inside, much of the available space was taken up by large, raised platforms. The dead were buried in these platforms, which were probably also used as work benches and as seats and beds.

The people of Catal Hüyük seem to have taken great care of their homes. They kept them fresh and clean by renewing the plaster on the walls each year. They were also careful about disposing of their rubbish. Certain courtyards were set aside as rubbish dumps, and the refuse was covered with wood ash to stop smells and deter rats.

MYSTERIOUS PLACES
THE MASTER BUILDERS

MYSTERIOUS PLACES
THE MASTER BUILDERS

Philip Wilkinson & Michael Pollard

Illustrations by Robert Ingpen

CHELSEA HOUSE PUBLISHERS
New York • Philadelphia

First published in the United States by
Chelsea House Publishers, 1994

First Printing
1 3 5 7 9 8 6 4 2

Simplified text and captions by **Michael Pollard**
based on the *Encyclopedia of Mysterious Places*
by Robert Ingpen and Philip Wilkinson.

Editor   Diana Briscoe
Designer   Design 23
Art Director   Dave Allen
Editorial Director   Pippa Rubinstein

ISBN 0-7910-2753-8

Printed in Italy

CONTENTS

Introduction

Everywhere we look, new buildings are being constructed and the builders seem to have a vast array of machines to aid them, from pile drivers to cranes.

Ancient builders had none of these machines, and yet they managed to create some extraordinary structures. One of the most famous is the stone circle at Stonehenge in southern England. It is made of enormous stone blocks, which the builders had to transport a long way to the site. And yet the people who built Stonehenge did not even have wheeled vehicles to help them carry the stones.

The same was true of the people who created the huge stone pyramids in many places in Central America, and the builders of the ancient temples on the island of Malta. How did they do it?

The builders' progress

This book shows how some of these mysterious buildings were created. It also explains why they were built – why people were prepared to put such great amounts of time and effort into making such strange structures. Some of the most basic buildings were made of simple materials that were easy to carry and use – the timber, straw and earth that were available near the site. And the reason they were made was the most basic of all – to give people shelter from the

rain and wind. The Iron-Age village of Biskupin in Poland shows how effective ancient buildings could be when created in this way.

But what if there was no local timber? In some places it was possible to use earth, making bricks out of mud and letting the warmth of the sun bake them hard. The buildings of the ancient Turkish town of Catal Hüyük were made in this way. Later on, bricks were baked in ovens.

An alternative was to use stone. At Skara Brae in the Orkney Isles, north of Scotland, stone was the only local material suitable for building. So the people made not only stone houses, but also stone furniture as well. Some of the stone cupboards and beds they made still survive.

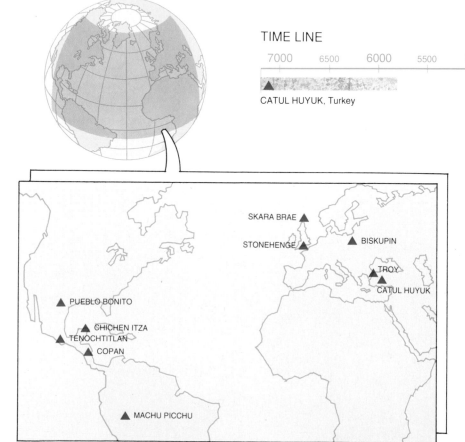

TIME LINE

| 7000 | 6500 | 6000 | 5500 | 5000 |

CATUL HUYUK, Turkey

SKARA BRAE

STONEHENGE   BISKUPIN

TROY

CATUL HUYUK

PUEBLO BONITO

CHICHEN ITZA
TENOCHTITLAN
COPAN

MACHU PICCHU

Power building

Biskupin and Skara Brae are good examples of how builders adapted to their surroundings, but they are hardly amazing feats of construction. Soon builders were using buildings as a deliberate way of showing something about their society. A building was more than a way of protecting its owners from the wind, rain or sun. It was a statement of the beliefs or attitudes of the people who lived in it.

You can see this change if you look at some of the later places in this book, especially Copan, Chichen Itza and Tenochtitlan. These were places dominated by their great stone pyramids. The pyramids were temples, designed by the priests who had a great deal of power. Their towering height showed people how important the priests and their ceremonies were. The lavish carvings and the complex inscriptions also reminded people of the priests' importance.

Both types of building – those made simply for shelter, and those made to make a point – are fascinating. When we look at them today we can learn a lot about the people who lived in and around them.

Both needed their master builders. These were the people who could plan the work, supervise the artists who created the decoration, and organize the often vast labor forces needed to move the stone and build the walls.

Philip Wilkinson

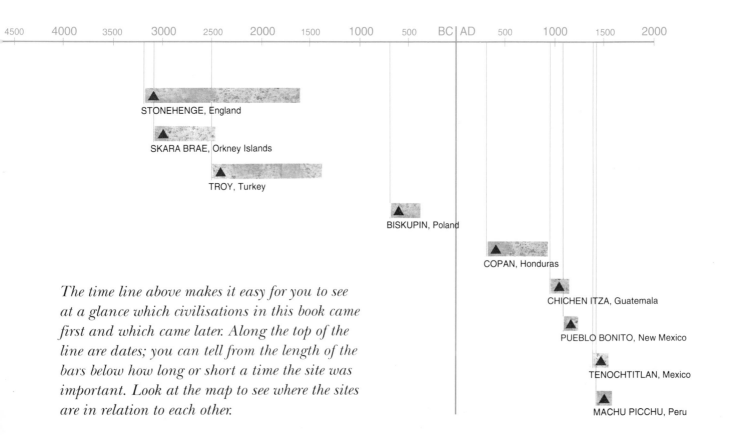

The time line above makes it easy for you to see at a glance which civilisations in this book came first and which came later. Along the top of the line are dates; you can tell from the length of the bars below how long or short a time the site was important. Look at the map to see where the sites are in relation to each other.

11

Measuring by hand

Although there was no written language in Catal Hüyük, the people seem to have worked out a system of mathematics which they used in building. They built most of their houses to standard sizes, usually about 20 feet (6 meters) long and 15 feet (4.5 meters) wide. Rooms, doorways, hearths, and ovens were also made to standard sizes.

The basic elements of their system of measurement were probably the human hand and foot. The standard mud brick was four hands long, two hands wide, and one deep.

Not all the buildings in Catal Hüyük were homes. There were also a large number of shrines built for religious ceremonies. These were decorated with paintings and sculptured clay panels which show that animals played an important part in the religion of Catal Hüyük. There were many hunting scenes, with deer being chased by leopards and human hunters. But the most prominent animals inside the shrines are plaster bulls, with real horns, mounted on the walls. It seems that to the people of Catal Hüyük, as to many other ancient civilizations, the bull was a symbol of life and action.

Sky burials

Other paintings in the shrines are more grisly. They show vultures picking the flesh off human bodies. The leader of the first excavation at Catal Hüyük, James Mellaart, believes that these pictures show how the people disposed of their dead. They gave them "sky burials."

The bodies of the dead were placed on tall platforms which kept them out of the way of animals such as dogs but allowed birds and insects to reach them. After the flesh had been stripped away, the skeleton would be brought down and buried beneath one of the platforms in the family's house or in a shrine. The women were buried under the larger platforms and the men under the smaller.

Female goddesses

Ancient civilizations like that of Catal Hüyük knew the importance of fertility of crops, animals, and human beings. They depended on fertility for survival.

This would explain the number of female goddess statues found in the ruins of the city. Some of them are shown to be pregnant and others actually giving birth, sometimes to human babies and sometimes to animals.

Archaeologists can only guess at what these statues meant to the people of Catal Hüyük. But birth means new life – for plants as well as animals – and it is likely that these statues were made in the hope that they would bring continuing new life to the soil and to the families of the city.

Carving of a fertility goddess.

Life in the city

Archaeology is slow, careful work. Excavations at Catal Hüyük have been going on for about forty years, but so far only part of the city has been uncovered. Our picture of life in Catal Hüyük is still far from clear.

One mystery is what work the people of Catal Hüyük did. We know that many of them were priests and priestesses, but what did the others do? The burial platforms in homes and shrines contain many grave goods (the possessions with which people were buried). These include fine examples of weaving, pottery, copper jewelry, weapons, baskets and wooden vessels. But so far little evidence has been found of where these objects were made. Some may have been brought from outside the city, but it is likely that the working area has still to be excavated. Much more of this intriguing city remains to be explored.

Fourteen cities

Another of Catal Hüyük's secrets is how long its civilization lasted. Although only a small part of the city has been excavated, fourteen different layers of buildings have been discovered, each layer built on the foundations of the previous one. But sadly, there is no way of knowing in detail the history of this mysterious city.

People of Catal Hüyük

Mainly by studying the skeletons and other contents of the burial platforms archaeologists have been able to find out a good deal about the people of Catal Hüyük, and especially about their skills.

They were taller than many other ancient peoples. The men were up to 5 feet 7 inches (1.7 meters) tall, and the women about 6 inches (15 centimeters) shorter. For those days, when there was no protection against disease, they had quite long lives. Men reached an average age of about thirty-four, and women about three years less.

What did they have to eat? Their diet included grain – probably made into a kind of porridge – and meat, and they drank milk, probably from sheep or goats.

Above: a stone stamp used for making patterns on the walls of a house.

Left: wall painting from a shrine showing vultures and a headless human.

A city of crafts

The big surprise about Catal Hüyük was the wide range of craft skills that its people developed.

One exciting discovery that the archaeologists made was a piece of cloth which had been used to fill a skull in one of the burial platforms. Although the cloth had been turned to ashes in a later fire, the pattern of the fibers could still be seen. This showed that the people of Catal Hüyük were expert spinners and weavers.

As well as cloth, they also wove mats out of rushes. The patterns made by these rugs can still be seen impressed in the clay floors of the houses. The patterns are like those used in rugs still made today in that part of Turkey.

The Catal Hüyük people knew about making dyes, too. They used plants such as woad to give a blue dye, madder for red and weld for yellow. Some of the wall paintings in the shrines still show traces of these colors. Many of these paintings are of animals, particularly bulls, stags and leopards; but there are also pictures of people hunting and dancing, of flowers and abstract patterns.

Catal Hüyük's secret skill

Simple domestic crafts like weaving could not have provided the wealth that a city like Catal Hüyük needed to grow and survive. It must have made some valuable product that it could trade with the outside world.

A clue to what this might have been is provided by the nearness to Catal Hüyük of two volcanoes. These produced a hard, glass-like volcanic rock called obsidian, which could be given a sharp edge for tools and weapons and could also be polished to make mirrors. The people of Catal Hüyük seem to have mastered the skills of grinding and polishing obsidian, as well as drilling

Household objects including a decorated boar's tusk.

tiny holes into it. It may be that their work was so specialized that the city was able to export finished articles made of obsidian in return for other goods.

Another material the craftsmen learned to work with was copper. Before 7000 BC they had found out how to use hammers to make simple tools and pins. A thousand years later they were smelting copper ore to make small beads and other items. But it was probably their skill with obsidian – a difficult material to work with – that brought wealth to the people of Catal Hüyük.

The finding of Catul Hüyük

The ruins of Catal Hüyük were found buried beneath a mound about 200 miles (320 kilometers) south of Turkey's capital city, Ankara. The archaeologist who discovered the mound and decided to investigate it was James Mellaart. He began to dig in 1961.

Mellaart and his team worked slowly and carefully, taking one section of the mound at a time. As each layer of earth was stripped away, Catal

Hüyük's secrets were gradually revealed.

By 1967 Mellaart was able to publish his first book about what he had found at this important but previously unknown site. This news of a city even older than those along the Tigris and Euphrates rivers, such as Ur and Babylon, made archaeologists rethink their ideas about the ancient world and the beginnings of civilization.

Stonehenge

England c. 3200–1650 BC

A great circle of stones has stood out against the sky on a hillside in southern England for 5,000 years. But how did it get there and why was it built?

Archaeologists have been trying to unravel the mysteries of Stonehenge for over 300 years. But even the modern equipment available today has been unable to answer all their questions.

The first thing you see as you approach Stonehenge is a circle of huge, upright stones. But there is more to Stonehenge than that. There are many other stones placed inside and outside the circle. There is also a bank, which archaeologists call an earthwork, surrounding the stone circle, and inside the earthwork a circle of pits which have been dug and then filled in.

The work of centuries

Modern techniques which enable us to work out the age of archaeological findings, reveal that Stonehenge was not built all at once, but in stages.

The earthwork is all that is left of the first stage. This was built between 3200 and 2700 BC. Then, the bank was much higher and wider than it is today – probably about 6 feet (2 meters) high and 20 feet (6 meters) wide. Inside it, there was a large wooden building, probably with a thatched roof, up to 100 feet (30 meters) across.

What happened inside this building? No one can be sure, but it may have been used to store the bodies of the dead before they were cremated or buried. Between 2700 and 2200 BC, a circle of fifty-six pits was dug inside the earthwork. Some of these holes contained the ashes of people whose bodies had been cremated. But the pits are older than the ashes, so they must have been dug for some other purpose. What could it have been?

Stone Age computer?

One idea is that the circle of pits was a kind of calculator designed to predict eclipses of the moon. This theory was put forward in the 1960s by Gerald Hawkins, an astronomer. He showed that if stones are placed on six of the holes in a certain pattern and then moved on one hole each year, the dates of future eclipses can be calculated.

We do not know whether the people of 2000 BC had the mathematical knowledge to make such calculations, but it seems unlikely. A more probable explanation of the pits is that liquids, possibly rain water, were poured into them as an offering to the gods of the underworld. But this too is only a theory. The circle of pits remains another of the mysteries of Stonehenge.

The first circle

Round about 2200 BC the first stones were brought to Stonehenge. They were arranged in a double circle inside the ring of pits. The mystery about this part of Stonehenge's history has to do with where the stones came from. They were "bluestones" from the Preseli mountains about 200 miles (320 kilometers) away in South Wales. There was plenty of other stone closer to Stonehenge that the builders could have used.

Why did they travel so far and go to the immense labor of transporting the stones all that way?

Finished at last

Between 2000 and 1600 BC the final stage of building was reached. This was the building of the circle of upright stones which now dominates the site. These huge stones rise to a height of

The people who built Stonehenge knew nothing about the wheel and did not use animals for haulage. All the work was done by human effort.

DID YOU KNOW?

13 feet (4 meters) and are buried up to 5 feet (1.5 meters) in the ground. Unlike the first stones, these came from the Marlborough Downs, only about 17 miles (27 kilometers) from Stonehenge, but transporting them must again have been a huge and difficult job.

When the great circle was finished, there were some more changes and additions. Groups of three even larger stones – two uprights and a lintel – were added in the centre, and the original bluestones were also moved to the centre. Work on Stonehenge then seems to have been complete.

Today, only about half of the stones are still in place. But Stonehenge still holds on to most of its secrets.

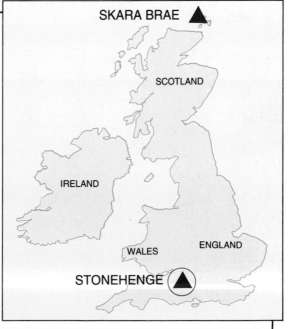

The remains of Stonehenge are on Salisbury Plain in England, about 70 miles southwest of London. Nearby are many other prehistoric remains which can also be visited.

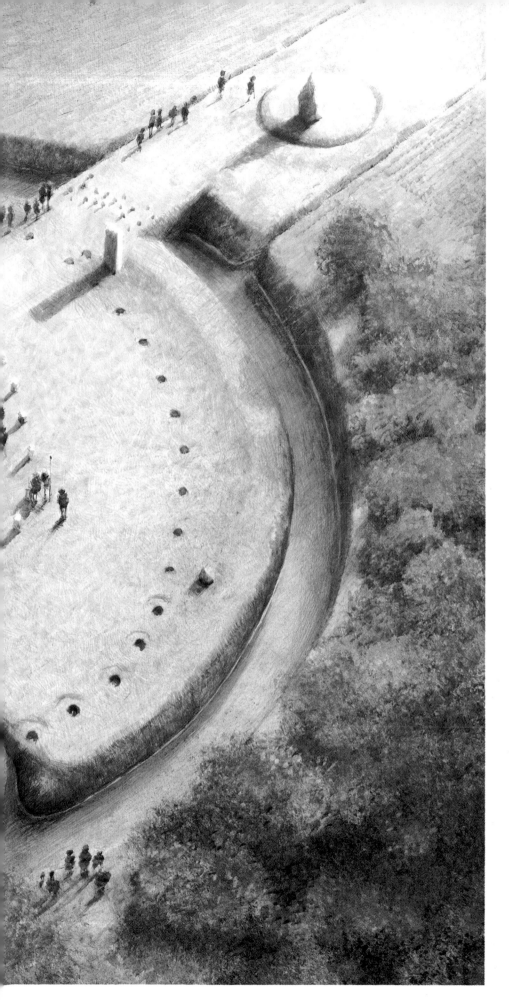

Midsummer dawn

It seems certain that Stonehenge was a center for religious ceremonies. It may also have been used to show off the power and skills of the people of the area. It was built with great care and accuracy, with the position of the pits and stones carefully worked out.

Stonehenge was built to last, as the centuries have shown. The stonemasons made sure that the lintels linking the upright stones were securely jointed. They were probably using skills they had learned as carpenters.

The rising sun

The most interesting thing about Stonehenge, and one which has fascinated people for centuries, is the way that the stones are arranged to make one particular day in the year important.

At the entrance to Stonehenge, just inside the embankment, is a stone called the Heel Stone. At dawn on Midsummer Day, June 24, the sun rises almost directly over the Heel Stone and points its shadow directly towards the great stone circle. We do not know what religious meaning this had for the people of Salisbury Plain thousands of years ago, but it is not hard to imagine them gathering before dawn and waiting in hushed silence for the sun to appear over the stone they had placed there for it.

Moving the stones

Even today, using cranes and trucks, bringing the stones to Stonehenge and placing them in position would be a major job. The people who built Stonehenge had nothing but their own strength and ingenuity to help them. Here is another of Stonehenge's mysteries – how did they manage?

We can only guess at the answer. It may be that the bluestones from South Wales were brought by sea and then by river, ending their journey on sleds which were dragged overland. But were Stone Age people able to build boats strong enough? How would they have loaded the stones on to the boats without sinking them?

Another idea is that, during the Ice Age, glaciers had carried the bluestones most of the way. But they would still have to be moved some distance across country, as were the stones from the Marlborough Downs. It has been shown that this could be done, using wooden levers and sleds, but it must have been a massive task involving thousands of people over a long period.

Then, once the stones had arrived, how were they erected, and how were

Stonehenge today.

Merlin

Stonehenge is so strange and old that it is not surprising that many myths and legends have grown up around it.

Some of these stories are about Merlin, who was said to have been the chief magician at the court of King Arthur, the legendary ruler of southern Britain.

Merlin was such a clever wizard, the story goes, that he could do anything. He took charge of the building of Stonehenge, which he made out of giants he had turned to stone. At Merlin's command, the stones would turn back into giants, and dance.

It is a good story, but the dates are all wrong. Merlin, if he really existed, was alive around the year AD 500, nearly 2,000 years after the building of Stonehenge was completed.

the lintels placed in position? Again, we do not know, but there are several possibilities. Earth ramps might have been used – but if so, there would still be signs that the soil had been disturbed, and there are none. The builders could have used a wooden scaffold – but it must have been immensely strong to take the weight of the stones, and no traces of a scaffold have been found. A third idea is that each stone was hauled up in stages, with a temporary wedge to hold it in place between each pull.

Whatever the answer really is, we can only admire the planning and effort that went into the task.

Skeleton of a man of the Beaker People, with a typical pottery beaker.

The Beaker People

The inhabitants of the country around Stonehenge at the time when the circle of pits was dug there are often known as "the Beaker People."

They get their name from a special kind of pottery jar. Many have been found in the graves of people who died around this time. Some archaeologists think that the beakers were used in religious ceremonies, perhaps to make offerings to the gods. This fits in with some ideas about the purpose of the circle of pits at Stonehenge.

At one time it was thought that the Beaker People were new settlers who arrived in the area. But it seems more likely that the beakers were merely a new style of pottery that began to be made about that time.

The Beaker People wandered far and wide in their search for pasture for their sheep and land which they could use for crops. In those days, the valleys were forested and could harbor wild animals or human enemies, so they traveled on higher ground along the ridges of the downs. Many of their tracks meet near Stonehenge.

John Aubrey

John Aubrey, born in 1626, was one of the first scholars to investigate Stonehenge. He discovered the circle of fifty-six holes inside the bank, which have since been called "the Aubrey holes."

But John Aubrey's guess at the age of Stonehenge was quite wrong. He thought that it had been built by the Celts, the people who lived in Britain when the Romans invaded in 55 BC. Many people continued to believe this until quite recently, but modern methods of dating have proved that Aubrey's guess was thousands of years off.

Skara Brae

Orkney Islands, c. 3100–2500 BC

*On the shore of a windswept Scottish island,
a storm revealed the remains of a village built about 5,000 years ago.
Who lived in this wild spot and why did they leave it?*

The storm that hit the Orkney Islands, off the north coast of Scotland, one day in 1850 was one of the worst anyone could remember. When it was over, the people of one of the islands, Orkney Mainland, discovered an unknown and mysterious chapter in their history.

Village by the sea

Among the sand dunes on the shore near the village of Sandwick the wind had blown the covering of sand away from the remains of an ancient village. There were about half a dozen houses, each between 15 and 21 feet (4.6 and 6.4 meters) across, with stone walls up to 6 feet (1.8 meters) thick. Around each house was a protective mound of earth. The houses had low doorways, but hardly any had window openings. The furniture inside was made of stone.

From each house door, a short passage led to a covered passageway which connected all but one of the houses. These passages were low, like the house doorways – only about 4 feet (1.2 meters) high.

Who were the people who had lived in this unfriendly place? Why did they leave their homes, and what happened to them?

Well equipped

One of the unusual things about the Skara Brae houses is how well they are equipped with furniture whose purpose we can easily understand today. There were shelf units similar to the dressers still found in many Scottish cottage kitchens – except that the Skara Brae units are made of stone. There are alcoves in the walls that were probably cupboards. There may have been a water supply in the form of storage tanks set into the floor, sealed with

Pieces of whalebone were found at Skara Brae, probably from dead whales washed up on the beach. What a find these huge creatures would have been for the villagers!

DID YOU KNOW?

*It was a hard life for the villagers of Skara Brae.
The weather was stormy, and the winters were bitterly cold. They wrapped themselves in furs
and built earth banks to try to keep the drafts out of their homes.*

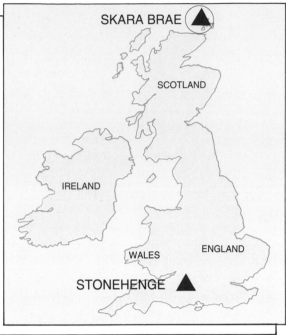

The remains of Skara Brae are on the west coast of Orkney Mainland, the largest of the Orkney Islands. This group of islands lie off the north coast of Scotland.

clay to make them watertight. The Skara Brae houses may even have had toilets. There are small stone areas leading off the main rooms, with a drain to the village passageway.

A world of stone

The people of Skara Brae were experts in the use of stone, of which the walls of their houses, and their stone furniture, were strongly and neatly made. The villagers made use of the material that was most easily found.

On the windswept Orkneys there are few trees, and wood was precious. It was kept for uses such as doors and roof supports where no other material would do. But there was plenty of stone.

What a load of rubbish!

It is not hard for a twentieth-century visitor to understand how the people of Skara Brae lived. But one fact about the village seems very strange to us today.

Skara Brae was built inside a mound which was actually an old rubbish dump (or midden), containing dung, bones, peat ash, and other rubbish. What is more, the houses themselves were filled with rubbish. Among other things, there were shells, antlers, and animal bones.

It seems strange that people, who in many ways seem to have lived such orderly lives, should have been content to live among their rubbish. But things become even more mysterious. First, the rubbish around the village is that of an earlier population. Why would people build their homes in their ancestors' rubbish dump?

Second, the rubbish inside the houses was not simply dumped there. It was arranged carefully in layers. The most likely reason why the village was built inside the midden of an earlier one is that it was easy to dig into. Within the mound there was shelter from the wind for the new houses. On this windy island, any extra protection from the weather was welcome. The explanation for the carefully layered rubbish in the newer houses is less easy.

Moving on

No one knows how the Skara Brae community came to an end, but at some time the houses were abandoned. As the village was very small, it may be that it was lived in by just one large, extended family.

Leaving a home is upsetting for anyone. In the harsh world of 2500 BC it must have been even worse. Some archaeologists have suggested that, to keep the family's link with its old home, the house may have been filled at some kind of ceremony with things connected with its owners. Sometimes these included the bodies or skeletons of dead members of the family.

We know nothing about the religion of Skara Brae, but perhaps the ash, shells, antlers, and bones were put there in memory of the old life of the houses. Perhaps the people, as they left their homes, could not bear to think of other people moving in and living there. Filling up the house in this way would certainly make it difficult for a new family to take over.

The end of Skara Brae

Why did the villagers of Skara Brae decide to leave their homes? It cannot have been a sudden decision caused by a violent storm or some other disaster such as an outbreak of disease. There was time to take the roofs off the houses and fill them with careful arrangements of bones and shells. It looks as if the decision to leave the village was planned well in advance.

We do not know the answer. Some time later, other people lived in the houses for a while until they, too, left. But all the people of Skara Brae went away in the end, leaving us to rediscover their homes and furniture 5,000 years later.

What did they eat?

We can tell, from the bones they left behind, that the people of Skara Brae were mainly meat-eaters. They raised sheep, cattle, and a few pigs. They were able to store enough feed to keep young sheep through the winter. The skins of their animals were used for clothes and bedding.

Hunting a wild boar.

Another important feature of the island's diet was fish. The battering of wind and waves has brought the sea nearer to Skara Brae than it was 5,000 years ago, but it was only a short walk to the shore. There, cod and other fish could be caught. The stone containers in the houses may have been stores for bait – possibly limpets – which have to be softened in fresh water before being used. There is little evidence of plants in the diet. Some grains and hazelnut shells have been discovered, but not enough to suggest that they were important foods.

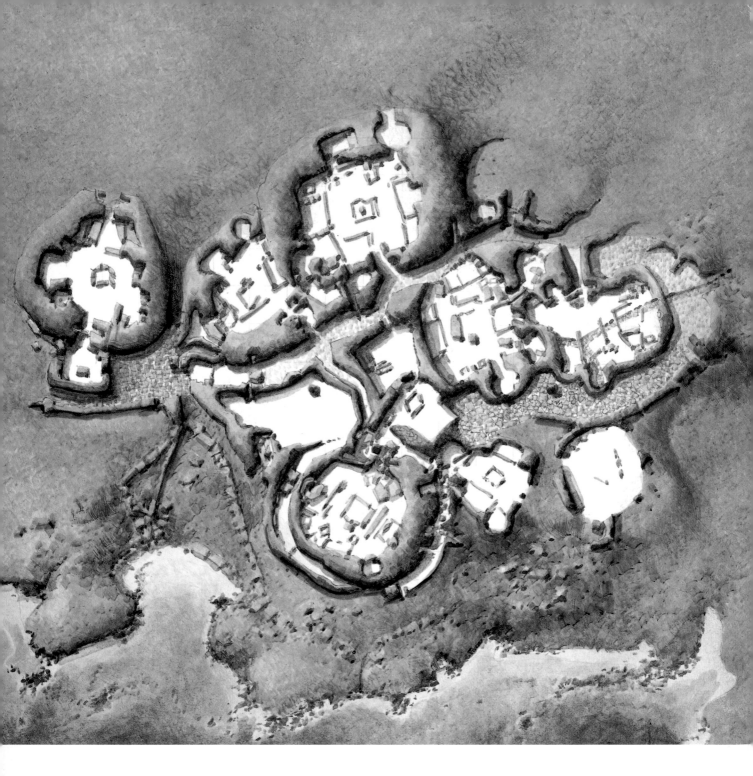

The village of Skara Brae

The ground plan of Skara Brae (above) shows the various houses and the connecting passageways. House 7 is at the bottom in the middle; House 8 is at the bottom right. House 7 was especially well preserved. From it, we can put together a fairly clear picture of what home life in the village was like.

To enter your house, you opened the low, narrow door which was held in place with a stone bar. Inside you would find a square room about 16 feet (5 meters) across. The floor was of beaten earth, but there was a paving of stone slabs round the doorway. In the center of the room was a square hearth, with four upright stone slabs to keep the fire in place. Peat was the fuel used in the fire. To one side was a raised area, which was probably used for preparing food and perhaps for eating.

Inside the house

Around the walls were stone box beds. These were frames made of stone slabs set on edge. They sound uncomfortable, but with a thick mattress of heather or straw to lie on, furs and skins as blankets, and the surrounding slabs to keep out the drafts they would have given the villagers a good night's sleep. Beds of a similar pattern, but with wooden frames instead of stone, were used on some remote Scottish islands until fairly recently.

The people of Skara Brae

Life at Skara Brae was hard. The villagers' main concern was with survival in a very hostile environment. Looking after their animals, making clothes, searching for food and keeping their homes in good repair would have taken up much of their time and effort. But some of them, at least, had time for various kinds of craftwork.

Some of this work produced everyday items such as pots. Although Skara Brae pottery was not very good in quality, its makers showed some artistic sense by decorating it with simple patterns such as zigzags and wavy lines. The villagers' work with carved bone showed more skill, and they included items made purely for pleasure, as well as small tools such as scrapers used to clean animal skins. Among the finds at Skara Brae are bone beads, decorative pins, and pendants, so some villagers must have had a liking for simple jewelry.

They also used their skill in working with stone to make hand tools and the mysterious carved objects that you can read about on the next page.

The village workshop

Stoneworking may have been carried on in a building specially set aside for it. House 8 at Skara Brae is the only building not connected to the main

Above: Bone beads, pendants and a dress pin.

Left: a leather cap.

passageway. It stands on its own at one end of the village. Like the homes, it has a hearth in the center of the floor, but there are no beds and none of the other domestic furniture that the homes have. Perhaps this was a workshop for the making of stone tools and other things. On the floor a large number of pieces of chert, a flint-like stone, were found. When it was heated in the fire, and then plunged into cold water, chert could be broken into flakes or splinters which were ideal as small cutting and shaping tools.

House 8 may have been one of a number of workshops for different crafts. There are traces of other buildings separated from the main block of homes around the edge of the village, but there is now no way of finding out what they were used for.

Mysterious carvings

It is not very hard to make simple tools out of stone, but some of the examples of stonecraft found at Skara Brae show that the villagers became very highly skilled at intricate stone carving.

These objects include stone balls with spiral designs carved on them, similar to those found in other places in the Orkney Islands and on the Scottish mainland.

But some objects are more cleverly made than those found elsewhere. One is an oval stone with double-pointed ends. Another is a ball covered with sharp spikes. It is hard to think of any use for these strange objects unless they had some religious meaning – though no one has been able to suggest what it was.

Some archaeologists think that the carvings on some of these stones may be an early form of writing. There are marks that look as if they have been arranged carefully in patterns of lines. Perhaps different patterns had different meanings.

There is no reason why the people of Skara Brae should have had a written language. They lived in a small village where they could communicate without writing to each other. The marks may be only decorations, like the patterns on Skara Brae pottery. But if they have any meaning, it could be some simple religious idea. For example, one pattern could represent one particular god.

Sadly, if the Skara Brae villagers were communicating with each other in writing, we will never know what they wrote.

Excavating Skara Brae

Excavations at Skara Brae began soon after the village was uncovered by the storm of 1850. But the major work on the site was done in 1928 and 1929 by a leading archaeologist of the time, Vere Gordon Childe.

Born in Australia, Professor Childe was an expert in prehistoric archaeology at Edinburgh University in Scotland. In 1928 he started work at Skara Brae, excavating another house and another section of the village passageway.

His discoveries added a great deal to our knowledge of Skara Brae, but he did not have today's equipment which makes it possible to date sites with great accuracy. Professor Childe believed that Skara Brae was a settlement of the Picts, a tribe who lived in the north of Scotland in Roman times. Modern radiocarbon dating of animal bones on the site have put the date of the village at between 3100 and 2480 BC, far earlier than Professor Childe could have guessed.

Troy

Turkey, c. 2500–1400 BC

*Everyone has heard of the ten-year war between the Greeks and the Trojans.
But what is the true story of the city that
held out for so long against an army determined to destroy it?*

The story of Troy is just one of the legends that have come down to us from Greek storytellers. Many of these legends were retold by Homer, a Greek poet who was writing before 700 BC, many centuries after the events he described had happened. No one knows how many of the legends about Troy are true, but they have become part of world history and literature.

When the ruins of ancient Troy were discovered about 130 years ago, archaeologists were keen to try to link their discoveries with the stories. Which of the cities built on the same site, they wondered, was the Troy that Homer wrote about?

The strange answer may be: two.

Fortress Troy

Troy II, as archaeologists call it, was a living city somewhere between 2500 and 1400 BC. Only about 300 feet (90 meters) across, it was more like a fortress than a city. Great watchtowers were set in its walls. It was clearly built to withstand attack. Among its houses, one – probably the ruler's – was much larger than the others.

It was in Troy II that Heinrich Schliemann, the archaeologist who led the first excavations of Troy in 1870, discovered the hoard of treasure that you can read about on page 41.

Death and destruction

Homer's story about the Siege of Troy ends with the city being destroyed by the Greeks. There was no sign that Troy II had been attacked, but when archaeologists excavated the remains of the later Troy VI they discovered signs of destruction and fire. So perhaps Troy VI was the city that was overcome at the end of the Trojan War – in other words, Homer's Troy.

Homer described a city on a hill in the middle of

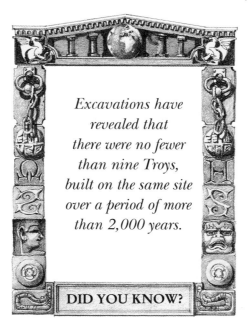

Excavations have revealed that there were no fewer than nine Troys, built on the same site over a period of more than 2,000 years.

DID YOU KNOW?

*The story goes that the Greeks gave the Trojans a huge wooden horse.
Unknown to the Trojans, there were Greek soldiers hidden inside. When night fell, the soldiers
climbed out and opened the city gates to let their army in.*

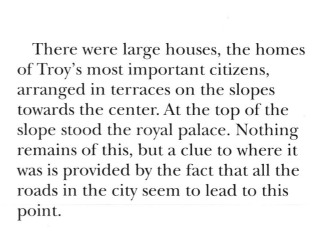

Troy lies about 6 miles (10 kilometers) from the Mediterranean end of the Dardanelles Straits which link the Mediterranean to the Black Sea. In ancient times the sea was much closer to the site.

a windswept plain. Its wide streets were enclosed by a solid wall. At the top of the hill stood the magnificent castle of King Priam, its walls lined inside with marble. Was this Troy VI? It was certainly a city which had met with some kind of disaster.

Priam's city?

Although Troy VI was bigger than the earlier cities, it was still quite small. It contained enough houses within the walls for about 1,000 people, though many more – perhaps up to 5,000 – may have lived outside the walls in wooden houses which have since vanished.

The walls were immensely strong. In one place, the foundations went down 23 feet (7 meters). They could have supported a watchtower over 65 feet (20 meters) high, which would have given the people of Troy good warning of any approaching enemies.

There were large houses, the homes of Troy's most important citizens, arranged in terraces on the slopes towards the center. At the top of the slope stood the royal palace. Nothing remains of this, but a clue to where it was is provided by the fact that all the roads in the city seem to lead to this point.

The mysterious fall of Troy VI

What happened to bring the life of this prosperous city to an end? If it was Homer's Troy and his story is true, it was wrecked by the Greeks after they had conquered it. But there is evidence that other forces were at work.

The catastrophe happened between about 1300 and 1250 BC. Some archaeologists think that the cause was an earthquake as the ruins are in one of the world's major earthquake zones. There are cracks in the walls that could have been caused in this way, but that may not be the whole story.

The ruins also show signs of fire damage. This might have been the result of the earthquake, when roof timbers crashed down on to hearths, or it could have been caused by an enemy attack. There are two sets of clues that suggest that such an attack took place. First, some of the damage to the walls looks more like the work of battering rams than of an earthquake. Second, a large number of weapons, probably Greek, have been found inside the walls.

Hard times

The people of Troy VI, who had the wealth and skills to rebuild, do not seem the sort to let their city just fall apart. But the next Troy was a much poorer place in which the people seem to have struggled to survive. The large houses were divided into smaller units, and there are few signs of wealth. So whatever happened in Troy VI seems to have destroyed the spirit of the people as well as many of the buildings.

The destruction of Troy

According to Homer's story, the Greeks slaughtered the leading citizens of Troy before ransacking the city. Perhaps, at the end of a long and bitter war, they damaged it so badly that it looked like the wreckage of an earthquake. They may have finished off the job by setting fire to the ruins.

This would have left the survivors – perhaps people who lived outside the walls and had been able to flee into hiding – with the task of carrying on their lives in the ruins. The wealth and leadership of the rich were no longer there to help them. This would explain why the city was never again as magnificent as Troy VI had been.

Real Trojan horses

Where did the wealth of Troy VI come from? Objects found in the ruins show that goods flowed into the city from Greece and Cyprus, as well as from places closer to home. Some of these were luxury items such as a gaming board, silver pins, beads made from ivory and carnelian (a semi-precious stone), pottery, and stoneware.

To obtain these goods, Troy VI must have traded other things in return, but there is less evidence of what these were. The city is said to have been famous for breeding horses, and these would have made a valuable export. The discovery of many horse bones on the site supports this idea. Many pieces of spinning equipment have also been found, so the Trojans might have made and traded in cloth. A third possibility is fishing. In the time of Troy VI the sea was closer to the city than it is now. Perhaps, too, Troy exported its own pottery, which has been found in Cyprus and the Middle East.

A Trojan coin.

City of dreams

The picture on the right is not a reconstruction of Troy as it really was. Instead, it shows how the Greeks imagined it from their legends and from Homer's description. Homer was writing centuries after Troy had been destroyed, so his picture of the city is also drawn from stories he had heard.

The long flight of steps leads to the royal palace among the trees, protected by a massive inner wall. The buildings with pillars supporting sloping roofs are temples to the Trojan gods.

Apart from what looks like a small market close to the nearest city wall, and perhaps a working area to the left of the picture, there is little hint of the trade that must have provided Troy with its wealth. This may have been carried on outside the walls.

The real Troy

In reality, as the excavations showed, none of the nine Troys had streets as wide as those in the picture. Nor, even at its most magnificent, did the city have so many impressive buildings.

To us, the real Troy VI – the largest of the nine – would seem small. It covered an area only about 650 x 390 feet (200 x 120 meters). If it is true that about 1,000 people lived inside the city walls, they must have lived in very crowded conditions.

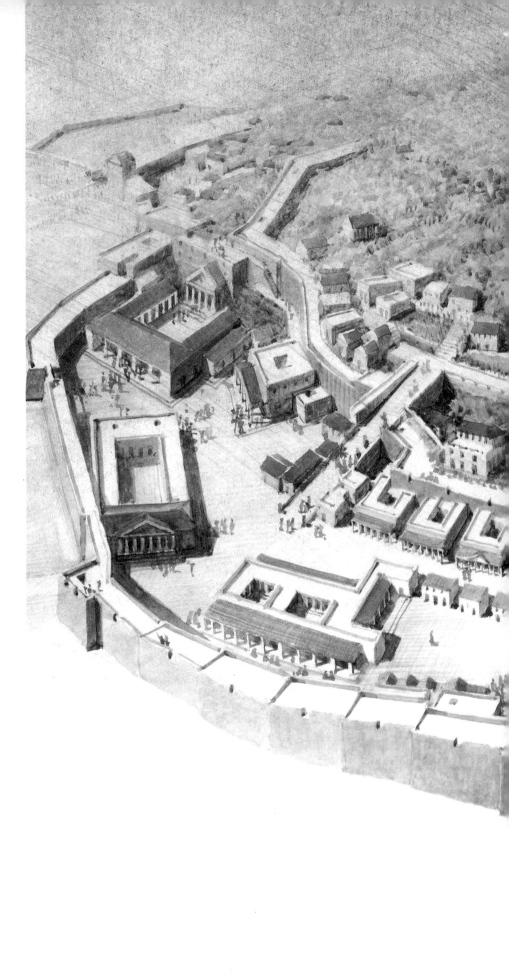

The Trojan Wars

According to Homer, the Trojan Wars began with a kidnap. The King of Sparta in Greece had a beautiful wife, Helen. Paris, the son of King Priam of Troy, fell in love with her and took her back to Troy.

This was the cue for an all-out Greek mission to rescue Helen and punish the Trojans. A great fleet of ships with warriors from all over Greece set out for Troy.

The Greeks expected a quick victory, but the fight proved harder than they had hoped. Landing on the coast, they reached the walls of Troy but were unable to break through. After a great battle, they surrounded the city and laid siege to it.

Stalemate

The siege continued for ten years. There were many battles but neither side gained the advantage. It began to look as if neither side could ever win. Then the Greeks had an idea. They built a huge wooden horse, large enough to conceal troops inside. The Greek fleet sailed away, leaving the horse behind on the shore.

The Trojans were delighted. They thought the horse was a peace-offering, and that the Greeks would trouble them no more. They hauled the horse through the city gates. At last, they thought, the long siege was over.

Darkness fell. As the Trojans celebrated the end of the war, the Greek ships sailed back under cover of night. Silently, Greek soldiers landed on the shore.

Their parties over, the Trojans went to bed. Then the doors of the wooden horse opened and the hidden Greek warriors jumped out. They crept to the city gates and opened them to let in their comrades. The siege of Troy was really over at last. Helen was reunited with her husband, and Troy was plundered and destroyed.

Greek and Trojan warriors locked in combat.

King Priam's treasure

One of the stories handed down from Greek legend is about the great storehouse of treasures belonging to King Priam of Troy. This story was very much in the mind of Heinrich Schliemann, the first archaeologist to excavate the mound that hid the ruins of Troy.

He was not disappointed. As he worked on the site of Troy II, he found vast hoards of valuable objects – precious stones, gold jewelry, cups and salvers. One gold diadem, or crown, was made up of over 16,000 separate pieces of gold. Schliemann told how he and his wife Sophie worked secretly to dig out and remove these treasures before local people could steal them. The finds convinced him that he had found King Priam's Troy.

Later archaeologists doubted Schliemann's claims. He might, they said, have collected the treasures from more than one level of the Troy cities. He might even have gathered them in different parts of the site and saved them up until he had enough to make a good story. Archaeologists do not always trust each other.

Mrs. Schliemann wearing some of Priam's treasure.

An amateur archaeologist

Originally a German merchant, Heinrich Schliemann took up archaeology as a hobby. He had not been trained and his methods of working were clumsy by today's standards.

Instead of working slowly and recording his finds, he dug straight into the middle of the mound that hid the remains of Troy. In doing so, he destroyed evidence that could have told us more about the city, and the records he kept of his work were confused. He was determined to find the Troy that Homer had written about, and every discovery convinced him that he had succeeded.

To be fair, Schliemann was working in the 1870s before archaeology had become a science. He had been led to the mound that was Troy by a careful reading of Homer, and when he started work, excitement took over from caution. He was careless, but he was the first to find the site and lead others to follow him.

The saddest part of the story is what happened to "King Priam's treasure." This and Schliemann's other finds were collected together in a museum in Berlin, but during World War II, they vanished. Unless they are found again some time in the future, the truth about their age will never be known.

Biskupin

Poland, c. 700–400 BC

*By a Polish lake, the people of Biskupin built their wooden houses,
with a sturdy wall to keep out intruders. But one of their most dangerous
enemies was in their own homes.*

Round about the year 720 BC, a group of people arrived by the shores of Lake Biskupin in central Poland. They were probably Slavs from the east. It would have been summer, as travelling through the bitter winter of central Europe was almost impossible.

They decided to make their homes beside the lake. There was a piece of marshy land jutting out into the water, and they chose this as the site. The fact that there was water on three sides, giving them protection from attack, might have helped them to make their choice.

Saved by mud

Lake Biskupin is a large stretch of water about 140 miles (225 kilometers) west of the Polish capital, Warsaw. In those days, the lake was smaller than it is now, and in the summer it may have shrunk to a watery bog.

If the people of Biskupin had not chosen this site for their village, we might never have known about it. Although the village was built entirely of wood, much of it was preserved when, years later, the lake grew in size and covered the houses with sand and mud. It was beneath these deposits that Biskupin was discovered in the 1930s.

Who were the enemy?

The people of Biskupin had chosen difficult land to work on, but perhaps the protection given by the water was more important to them. To make doubly sure of their safety, they surrounded the village with a wall 20 feet (6 meters) high and 10 feet (3 meters) across. It was a double wall made of wood, with earth filling the space between. The only opening was a single gate, probably with some kind of watchtower above it, on the landward side.

For people whose main activities were farming

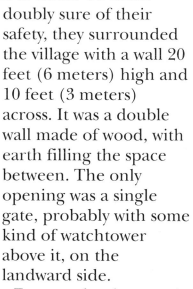

We know a lot about how the people of Biskupin lived, but nothing about what happened to them when they died. No human remains have ever been found.

DID YOU KNOW?

*The Biskupin villagers had a strong sense of cooperation
and teamwork. Here, they are working together to rebuild a house damaged by fire.
The houses were so close together that a fire could spread very fast.*

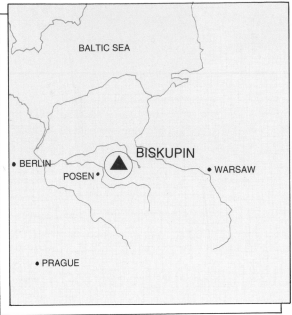

The reconstruction of the village of Biskupin is on Lake Biskupin, about 40 miles (65 kilometers) east of Poznan, a large city in the west of Poland. There is also a museum.

and craftwork, this seems like a lot of effort to make to defend themselves. What were they afraid of? There are no signs that Biskupin was ever attacked. But other walled villages, not as well preserved, have been found in Poland. Probably any prosperous village like Biskupin was at risk from robbers.

Houses on stilts

As the ground was so soft, the builders had to sink supports deep into the marsh to keep the houses upright. They also paved the ground between the houses with logs so that people could move about more easily.

About one hundred houses were packed inside the wall in an area of about 5 acres (2 hectares). They were built in long rows side by side, rather like a terrace of houses today, with log pavements between them. There was a wooden road running round the village just inside the wall. Building houses in rows, which used less wood and space,

and took less time, than if the houses were separate, is interesting because it shows that the people of Biskupin must have been well organized and willing to work together on a community project.

Damp-proofing

Most of the houses had one large room, though some were split into two. They had wooden floors which rested on layers of birch sticks to stop dampness creeping up from the marshy land below. Each house had a stone hearth covered with a layer of clay to cut down the risk of fire.

The winters in this part of Poland were harsh, with heavy snow and biting winds from the east. The lake and marsh were frozen over for several months on end. There would be little activity out of doors at that time of year. In such a climate, building houses in rows, so that most of them had only two outside walls, would have helped to conserve heat.

Keeping themselves to themselves

The variety of objects found at Biskupin shows that the people there lived full, active lives. They kept cattle, sheep, pigs, and goats. They plowed the land nearby and grew wheat, barley, and some kind of beans. They also made things. Spindles and loom weights for spinning and weaving have been found, together with leatherworking tools and evidence of metalworking, at first in bronze and later in iron.

There are some signs that trade was carried on. Amber and glass beads found at Biskupin may have come from the Baltic, and other objects came from Hungary and Italy. But it is highly unlikely that the village was an important trading center. It is possible that traders from other places passed by and exchanged goods.

The lives of the Biskupin people seem to have been very much rooted in their own community and they would perhaps have been put off exploring by the dangers of travel and trade.

Escaping the flood

Wooden buildings, especially in a harsh climate, need constant repair. We do not know how long the village of 720 BC lasted, but it seems that at some point, some houses had fallen down or been demolished.

By 560 BC, Biskupin was slightly smaller. One street had disappeared and the original houses had been replaced by smaller ones which were less well built. They were possibly sited at a higher level above the marsh, and it may be that the level of the lake was already rising.

If this happened in winter, it must have been a severe blow to the population, who would have had to build new shelter quickly. This could explain why the later houses were evidently put up in a hurry.

In the end there was no escaping the waters of the lake. They flooded the site and it had to be abandoned – but it was the rising water that preserved Biskupin for us to see today.

Victim of war

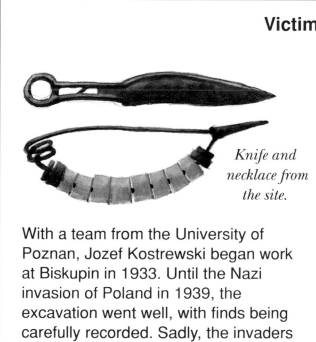

Knife and necklace from the site.

destroyed the team's records and even some of the finds, so that our knowledge of Biskupin can now never be as good as it might have been.

When peace came, the Polish archaeologists returned and continued their work. They have since reconstructed some of the buildings so that visitors can see what the original settlement was like.

With a team from the University of Poznan, Jozef Kostrewski began work at Biskupin in 1933. Until the Nazi invasion of Poland in 1939, the excavation went well, with finds being carefully recorded. Sadly, the invaders

A wooden plow.

The worst enemy

Although the people of Biskupin believed that there were enemies outside their village wall, their greatest enemy was inside. It was fire.

The entire village – even its roads and pavements – was built of wood. Every house had its hearth, and in some buildings the fires had to be stoked up to reach the high temperatures needed for metalworking. Fire was an ever-present risk, and evidence has been found that

Biskupin was several times partly destroyed. It is easy to imagine how panic would spread along the rows of houses if fire broke out in one of them. The buildings were so tightly packed together that any fire could easily have wiped out the entire village.

Perhaps it was the knowledge that they all depended on each other that bound the community tightly together. If they were to

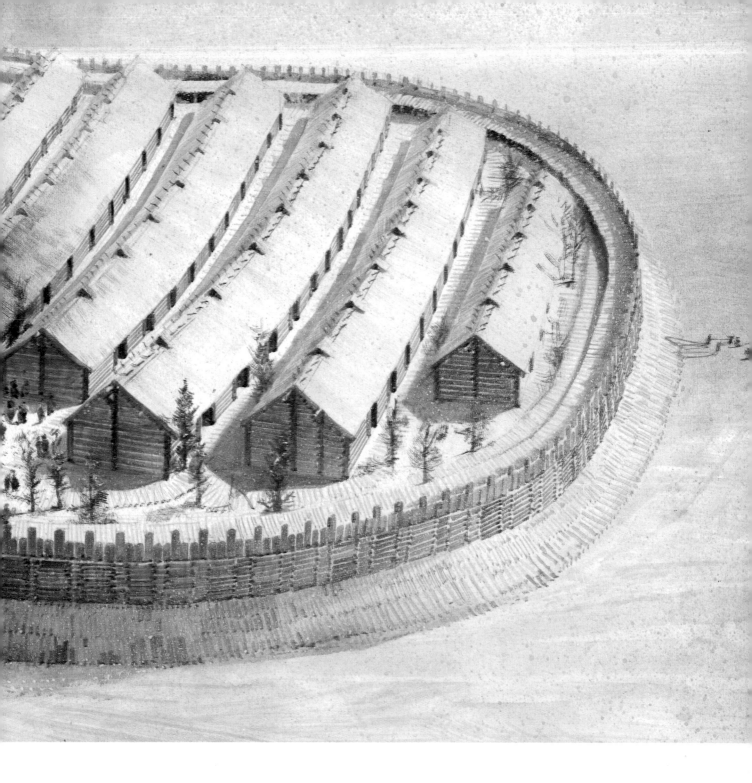

survive as a village, they had to work together to stop fires spreading and to repair any damage. In the picture above they are rushing to put out a fire in one of the houses. It is not hard to imagine them forming a human chain to pass containers of water from the lake.

But this kind of teamwork usually needs a leader to organize it. In most ancient settlements there was a leader or chieftain, whose home stood out because it was larger than the others. There is no sign of a chieftain's house at Biskupin. Perhaps the village leader lived in the same kind of house as everyone else. It may be that the village was ruled by someone living outside. Although we can understand a lot about life at Biskupin from the objects found there, we know nothing about how its society worked or even what language they spoke.

Copan

Honduras, c. AD 300–900

At the top of the pyramids, high above the city of Copan, human and animal sacrifices were carried out in the hope of pleasing the gods and bringing prosperity.

Copan was built by the Maya people, a civilization that flourished in Central America between AD 300 and 900. It was an advanced civilization in many ways: it had a written language and used a calendar similar to ours. The Maya were also expert craftsmen in stone. However, there were strange gaps in their knowledge.

They knew about the wheel and used it on toys – but they had no wheeled transport and did not use wheels to make pottery. They were good arable farmers, but they did not raise animals. They hunted wild animals for their meat. Although in their later years they discovered how to work with metal, they used it only for decorative things and continued to make tools and weapons out of stone.

Worship and war

The two most important things in the life of the Maya were religion and war. Both were bloodthirsty.

The Maya cities fought savagely among themselves, and their battles ended with the beheading of the leaders of the losing side. Prisoners of war became slaves.

From early childhood, boys were trained for war. They were taken to live away from their families and taught to paint themselves black, the color of Maya warriors. When they returned to their families, they married and exchanged their war paint for colorful body decorations and tattoos.

The Maya religion involved human and animal sacrifices, and ceremonies in which they tortured their own bodies. It seems that the Maya gloried in the sight of blood.

City in the forest

Copan was built about AD 725 in a clearing in the upland forest of what is now Honduras.

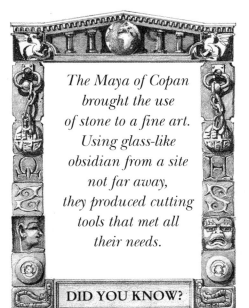

The Maya of Copan brought the use of stone to a fine art. Using glass-like obsidian from a site not far away, they produced cutting tools that met all their needs.

DID YOU KNOW?

A sacred ball game, played on a special court, was part of the religion of the people of Copan. This picture, based on carvings found at Copan, shows one of the players dressed for action.

Copan is in Honduras in central America, very close to the border with Guatemala. It is about 145 miles (225 kilometers) north-west of the capital Tegucigalpa.

Its centerpiece was a collection of temples and pyramids set on a raised stone platform. Below this were the city's houses, which were built of wood and have long since disappeared. Copan was a large city, with many thousands of homes.

Good and bad days

Among the most important people among the Maya were the scribes. They were the scholars of Maya society. At least some of them were also priests. This double role gave them great power.

They were especially good mathematicians and astronomers. It was the scribes who worked out the Maya calendar, which you can read about on page 54. They were also responsible for keeping the records of Maya history.

To the Maya, the calendar was much more than a way of telling what day it was. It was closely linked with their religion. They believed that the days were gods, some bringing good times and others bringing disaster. There were also gods linked to the success of farming, such as the corn god and the rain god. It was to please these gods that sacrifices were made.

History in stone

The history of their people was important to the Maya. It brought together the ideas of time and religion.

The plaza or public square below the pyramids of Copan were dotted with stone *stelae* or pillars. On these was carved writing telling stories of Maya history and also the religious meaning of the calendar. The *stelae* were richly illustrated with pictures of the gods, who had lifelike faces and bodies decorated in great detail.

Stone was not the only material the Maya used for their writing. They also wrote on animal skins and paper made of bark.

The fight to survive

Providing the essentials of life for a city of several thousand people, using very basic tools, was hard work, but the Maya were very active people.

They were enthusiastic arable farmers, cutting down the forest to make way for crops. Tree-felling must have been difficult without metal tools, and without wheeled wagons to haul the felled trees away. Once they had cleared the land, the farmers grew corn, beans, squashes – pumpkin-like vegetables – and chilies. In the remaining forests hunters caught deer and wild pigs, using darts, snares, and traps.

The Maya had an unusual method of fishing. They put drugs, such as the leaves of the fish-fuddle tree, in the water to stun the fish so that they could be easily caught.

What happened to Copan?

The Maya civilization was gradually overtaken, from around AD 900, by the more powerful Toltec people. But there is no sign that the Toltecs ever attacked Copan.

It seems that at some point the city began to lose its prosperity, and its people drifted away to new homes. The quick-growing tropical forests reclaimed the land that the Maya had used for farming, and it was deep in thick forest that the ruins of Copan were discovered about 800 years later. But it was not the end of the Maya people. Their descendants still live in parts of Guatemala and Honduras.

Plodding along

It is strange that, in spite of their grasp of practical skills such as building and their understanding of mathematics, the Maya people did not use wheeled transport or discover the use of the wheel for making pottery. Yet they knew about wheels and used them on toys. Somehow they failed to apply this knowledge to other things.

Trucks and wheel barrows would have been of great help to them in their huge building work. It may be that because they had a plentiful supply of slaves to do heavy carrying and lifting work, they saw no need to make these tasks easier.

As there was no contact between the Maya and civilizations in other continents, they knew nothing of the wheeled transport that had been used in Babylon 5,000 years before.

There were no horses or cows in the Americas before the Spanish arrived in 1519. So the Maya had no pack animals either and relied on people power.

Wheeled toy from a Mayan tomb.

Death in the sky

Sacrifices and other religious ceremonies took place in the temples at the top of the pyramids which were dotted about Copan. Unlike Egyptian pyramids, those of the Maya civilization were built in stepped layers, with a long flight of steps leading up to the top. The religious center of Copan, seen here, is the only part to have survived.

Only scribes and a few other privileged people were allowed to climb the steps to the temples. Here, sweet-smelling incense was burned as the religious ceremonies were carried out.

Human sacrifices were attended by four men who were called chacs. *Their job was to hold down the victim. But the sacrifice was not always human; dogs, squirrels, iguanas or birds were sometimes killed instead.*

Looking into the future

Another ceremony performed in the pyramid temples involved a soothsayer or prophet, called a chilam, *who would go into a trance and foretell the future.*

These ceremonies would be watched by the people of Copan who gathered in the square below. The shape of the pyramids would have concentrated their attention and led their gaze upwards to what was happening at the top. Viewed from below, it must have seemed that the temples were up in the sky.

Experts on time

The Maya calendar, like ours, was based on the time that the earth takes to complete its journey round the sun. The scribes were able to calculate this very precisely. They made it 365.2420 days, which is only two-thousandths of a day (or just under three minutes) different from the most modern scientific calculations.

The Maya divided their year into 20 periods of 18 days each. As this made 360 days, five days were left over at the end of the year. These days "outside the calendar" were called the *haab,* and they had a special meaning for the Maya.

Days of danger

As the other 360 days all belonged to particular gods, the five days of the *haab* were particularly dangerous. The Maya took care not to fall asleep in daylight on these days, not to quarrel with anyone, and not to stumble or trip. If they could, they stayed at home and refused to do any work that they did not like. Only when the new year started was it safe to resume their normal lives.

The calendar had an important practical use in planning the sowing and harvesting of the farmers' crops. But Maya culture and religion were also closely tied to time. The Maya believed that time moved in a circle and that history repeated itself. Periods of war and political upheaval would occur regularly and could be predicted from what had happened in the past. Their calculations ranged from up to 400 million years into the past, and up to 4,000 years ahead.

The scribes' study of the calendar produced some remarkably accurate forecasts of the future. One, for example, predicted the arrival of white men. In the 16th century, this is exactly what happened. Europeans arrived, and the old civilizations were destroyed.

Above: symbols from a Mayan calendar.

A Mayan scribe.

The Olmecs

The Maya borrowed many of their beliefs from the Olmec civilization, which flourished in Central America from 1200 BC to about AD 400.

The first people to live in the area were probably from North America.

A huge Olmec stone head.

They had travelled from the north and moved from place to place as they hunted for their food. About 1500 BC these people began to settle in villages and farm the land around them. Their villages grew into towns, and this was the start of the Olmec culture.

The Olmecs lived in an area where there was little stone, so they used clay for their buildings, including the pyramid temples. Towards the end of the Olmec civilization the people developed a calendar and a method of writing. The language was similar to that of the Maya, and many of the features of their religion, such as the importance attached to the jaguar, continued into Maya times.

The Olmec civilization did not develop as far as building cities, though the village which grew into the city of Copan under the Maya was probably founded by the Olmecs. The earlier culture laid the foundations of a civilization on which the Maya, with their greater skills and better resources, were able to build.

Lost in the jungle

Copan was first discovered in the 1830s by Colonel Juan Galindo. In 1839 two American explorers who specialized in the civilizations of Central America, John Stephens and Frederick Catherwood, made the first excavations there. But it was not until the 1880s that another American, Percival Maudslay, surveyed the site properly for the first time and made many new discoveries.

Between the visit of Stephens and Catherwood and that of Maudslay, photography had been invented. Maudslay was one of the first people to show how valuable the camera could be as an archaeological tool. His collection of pictures provides a record of what the ruins of Copan looked like as he uncovered them. Between 1935 and 1947 there were more excavations with American sponsorship, and some of the ruins were restored.

The legendary Quetzalcoatl

A huge and strange creature, half serpent and half bird, is the hero of many of the stories of the Central American civilizations. Its name is Quetzalcoatl (pronounced Kwet-sal-co-at-el) or Kukulcan. The stories of Quetzalcoatl began long before the time of the Maya, but they took them over as part of their own religion.

In the stories, Quetzalcoatl is the creator of law and knowledge and the inventor of the calendar. He taught people everything that they knew, including how to farm, weave and make pots. He showed the human race that corn was good food. Changing himself into a black ant, he stole some corn from the red ants and showed humans how to plant it.

Is the story of Quetzalcoatl based on a real person who at some time lived in Central America? We can only guess at the answer. It seems likely that there were a number of great rulers who each added something to Central American culture. Over the years, memories of these rulers were joined into one. Perhaps the idea was that Quetzalcoatl – who could change himself into anything he chose – inhabited each of these men in turn.

In one way, Quetzalcoatl was very different from the people who worshiped him. He was a kind leader who hated to hurt any living creature and who would not allow any but the smallest sacrifices to be made to him. By the time Copan was built, this side of Quetzalcoatl had been forgotten.

One of the myths about Quetzalcoatl was an explanation of night and day. In this story, Quetzalcoatl was the son of the Sun and Moon. As he grew up, he discovered that he had enemies – the stars of the Milky Way – who were determined to kill Quetzalcoatl's father. They succeeded, and buried the Sun's body in sand.

Vultures came to Quetzalcoatl, who was then nine years old, and told him what had happened. Helped by animal friends, he found the body and brought his father back to life.

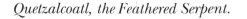

Quetzalcoatl, the Feathered Serpent.

Tezcatlipoca

In most religions, different figures represent good and evil. In Central America, Quetzalcoatl, the son of the Sun and Moon, represented good. His main enemy was Tezcatlipoca (pronounced Tes-cat-li-po-ca), who was the god of the night and whose 400 star sons in the Milky Way had hunted down and killed the Sun, who was a god called Ah Kinchil. Tezcatlipoca then set out to destroy Quetzalcoatl himself and banish good from the world for ever.

Like Quetzalcoatl, Tezcatlipoca could change his appearance whenever he liked. He could also change the appearance of other gods. His own favorite disguise was that of a turkey, a bird which is native to Central and South America. In place of one of his feet he had a mirror, and it was this that helped him bring about Quetzalcoatl's downfall.

Mischief with a mirror

First, he changed Quetzalcoatl into an ugly creature with wrinkled skin and sunken eyes, and made him look in the mirror. Quetzalcoatl was so ashamed of his appearance that he hid himself away from the world.

Then Tezcatlipoca came again and

Tezcatlipoca, god of night.

changed his enemy into a beautiful creature dressed in the finest clothes. Quetzalcoatl wore a robe made of green feathers and a splendid turquoise mask. Looking in the mirror, he felt that he was once again fit to go out into the world.

Death before dishonor

This was the wily Tezcatlipoca's chance to finish him off. He organized a party at which Quetzalcoatl drank so much wine and behaved so badly that when he awoke the next day he was filled with shame and decided to kill himself.

He ordered his servants to build him a funeral pyre on the beach. Meanwhile, he dressed himself in his feathered robe and turquoise mask. When the pyre was lit, he threw himself on it and the flames destroyed him. But as he burned, the ashes rose from his body as a flock of birds, carrying his heart with them. They flew high into the sky and Quetzalcoatl's heart turned into the planet Venus.

The story says that when Venus appears each evening, it shows that Quetzalcoatl is still on his throne, shining the light of goodness down upon the world. So the whole story – the death of the Sun and the coming to life of Venus – is replayed over and over again every night.

Chichen Itza

Mexico, c. AD 950–1150

*The Toltec city of Chichen Itza was strange and sometimes sinister.
Why were more than 40 people, half of them children, thrown down the sacred well?
What was the purpose of the* caracol, *with its spiral staircase?*

After the Maya civilization faded away, for reasons we do not know, a new culture took its place in Central America. The newcomers, known as the Toltecs, built splendid cities, of which Chichen Itza in Mexico was a fine example, although it was only their second city. Their capital was Tula, nearly 750 miles (1,200 kilometers) away across the Gulf of Mexico.

City of death

In some ways, Chichen Itza is like Copan. There are similar paved squares or plazas, similar pyramid temples, a ball court and many stone carvings. But life at Copan, compared with Chichen Itza, seems quite calm and peaceful. To judge by the carvings, the Toltec filled their lives with war, death and human sacrifice.

Images of the serpent

Like the Maya, the Toltec people worshiped a god called Quetzalcoatl (see pages 56–57), and the image of the feathered serpent appears time and again in their sculptures and in the stone columns of the main buildings of Chichen Itza.

But the Toltec Quetzalcoatl had a different character from the god of the Maya. He was more warlike and demanded more human sacrifices. One story is that Chichen Itza was ruled by a king who called himself Quetzalcoatl, perhaps to make himself popular. But he was a fierce warrior and cruel tyrant, quite unlike the god whose name he had taken. This would explain why the Toltec Quetzalcoatl seems to have presided over a reign of terror.

The Fifth Sun

One clue to how Quetzalcoatl became linked with human sacrifice is provided by one of the Quetzalcoatl myths. This tells the story of the fifth sun.

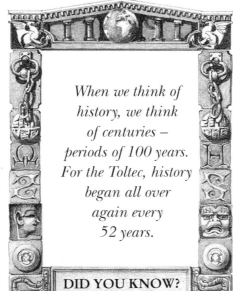

When we think of history, we think of centuries – periods of 100 years. For the Toltec, history began all over again every 52 years.

DID YOU KNOW?

The procession at the top of the picture is passing a chacmool, *or altar figure, which is waiting to receive the heart of a human sacrifice. Below a sculpture of Quetzalcoatl broods in the darkness of the old temple.*

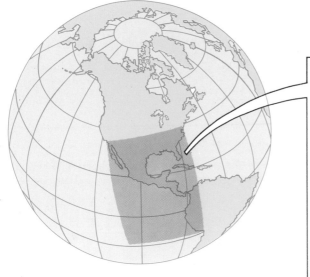

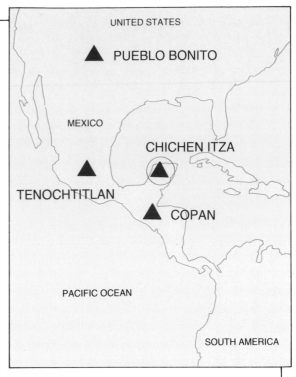

Chichen Itza is in the Yucatan peninsula of Mexico, just west of a town called Valladolid and about 75 miles (110 kilometers) east of a larger town called Merida.

The legend went that the sun that the Toltec knew was the fifth one. Four earlier suns had been destroyed in turn by jaguars, fire, wind, and water. Each time, the earth returned to darkness.

Quetzalcoatl made the fifth sun, and gave light and life back to earth, by sacrificing himself and giving his heart and blood. The Toltec may have continued to offer human hearts and blood as sacrifices in the hope that these would enable the fifth sun to survive.

The temple of Quetzalcoatl

The main temple of Quetzalcoatl in Chichen Itza was a large pyramid in the centre of the city which is known today as the Castillo. It stood 78 feet (24 meters) high, and on each of its four sides there was a stairway leading to the temple at the top. Each stairway has 365 steps – one for each day of the year – and the pyramid itself has nine steps or terraces, one for each of the nine regions of the underworld in Toltec myth. The outside is decorated with masks of gods and carvings showing Toltec warriors.

Inside the pyramid mound that the archaeologists excavated first, they found another. In the Toltec culture, the life of a temple was 52 years. At the end of that time, they either demolished it and put up another or, as at Chichen Itza, built a new one round the old. Among the treasures in the inner temple was a stone throne in the shape of a jaguar, with eyes of jade – a semi-precious stone – and teeth made of shell.

The sacred well

One of the grimmest finds that archaeologists made at Chichen Itza was the *cenote* or sacred well. It is thought that people were thrown into it in times of drought to please the rain-god Tlaloc (pronounced T-lal-ok). When the well was excavated, the skeletons of 42 people were found, of which 20 were children. There were also pieces of jade and gold medallions with pictures of Toltec warriors.

Archaeologists say that we should read the evidence of the sacred well with care. Although human sacrifices were part of Toltec culture, the skeletons in the well date from a later time. But the gold medallions are clearly linked with the Toltecs.

The mysterious "snail"

Of all the buildings at Chichen Itza, the most unusual is the *caracol*, or snail, so called because of its spiral staircase.

The *caracol* is the only circular building that has so far been found in the Maya or Toltec cities. Its spiral staircase is also unusual for these cultures. Archaeologists think it may have been an observation tower used by scribes to study the stars and check the calendar. Probably it was also a watchtower from which guards could warn of approaching enemies.

What happened at Chichen Itza?

What became of Chichen Itza is as much of a mystery as what happened to Copan. Both cities seem to have simply faded away for no real reason.

We know that the Toltecs' main city, Tula, was destroyed by fire around AD 1200. But there is no sign that such a disaster befell Chichen Itza, and no sign either that the city was attacked. Yet Chichen Itza began to decline in importance at about the same time.

It may be that once Tula had been destroyed, there was no future for the second Toltec city. We know that there was a good deal of trade between the two, and perhaps Chichen Itza could not survive without this. Whatever happened, neither their sacrifices to their gods nor the strength of their warriors could save the people of the city from the tide of history.

Cave of the rain god

The sacred well was not the only place in Chichen Itza dedicated to the rain god Tlaloc.

About 2.5 miles (4 kilometers) to the east of the city is a cave system with an underground stream. Water drips steadily from the ceiling, having filtered through the rock above. Perhaps the damp atmosphere made this a natural place for offerings to be made to Tlaloc. After all, it would be easy to imagine a rain god feeling at home there.

The people of Chichen Itza brought to the cave dozens of incense burners made of pottery or stone. Some of them were in the shape of Tlaloc's head. They were placed at various points through the cave system. Unusually for the Toltecs, this was a bloodless tribute; there is no sign of human sacrifices.

Pot showing the head of Tlaloc.

A hub of activity

This reconstruction shows the sacred buildings at the heart of Chichen Itza around AD 1180, before the city began to decline.

The tall, round building in the centre is the caracol, *with its internal spiral staircase. It stands about 400 feet (122 meters) high. The tall pyramid to the left is the Castillo, the temple to Quetzalcoatl. Beyond, in the middle distance, the Temple of the Warriors, celebrating the Toltec people's warlike nature, stands on its smaller pyramid.*

A corner of the court where the sacred ball game was played can just be seen on the left of the picture.

The city was mainly a place where ceremonies took place, and where the priests and military leaders lived. Farmers and craftsmen and their families lived some distance away in small villages near the land they worked on.

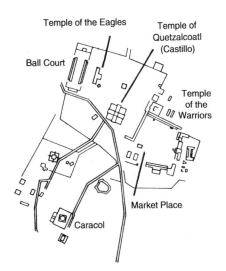

Temple of the Eagles

Temple of Quetzalcoatl (Castillo)

Ball Court

Temple of the Warriors

Market Place

Caracol

A deadly serious game

The importance the Toltecs attached to their ball game is shown by the carefully-planned arena they built for it. It is similar in some ways to a modern soccer ground except that there is no seating.

The playing area measured 420 x 197 feet (128 x 60 meters). This is not very different in size from a modern, full-size soccer field. The court was surrounded by a wall 26 feet (8 meters) high. Beyond the wall there was a viewing platform for the important citizens of Chichen Itza, just as important visitors to soccer matches today have special places where they can get a good view of the play. Lesser folk had to watch the game from the terraces of nearby temples.

Playing for their lives

Two teams played the game with a solid, rubber ball. The aim was to score goals by passing the ball through stone rings placed

The ball court ai Chichen Itza with a game in progress.

high on each side of the court. The rules of the game made scoring particularly difficult. Players were not allowed to let their hands or feet touch the ball. They had to move it with their shoulders, arms or knees.

It must have been a hard game to play, but each side probably had a great incentive to win. The locals told the Spanish invaders that the losers in Aztec games were sacrificed to the gods (see Tenochtitlan).

Skull relief from the ball court.

Warlike city

Scenes of battle and processions of warriors were among the most common subjects of the carvings at Chichen Itza. A period of service in the army was compulsory for all men. Yet if these warriors ever went into action, it must have been well away from Chichen Itza. There is no sign among the ruins that battles were ever fought there.

The Temple of the Warriors, built to glorify war, is one of the great buildings of the city center of Chichen Itza. There is a platform from which a stepped pyramid rises, with the temple at the top. Round the platform is a low building with its roof held up by columns, and it is these columns that give the temple its name. They are decorated with carvings of Toltec soldiers. The soldiers wear butterfly-shaped breastplates and bands of feathers on their heads, and have earrings and nose ornaments. Their weapons are javelins and spears.

Inside the temple on top of the platform are more warriors – but the columns at the entrance carry a feathered serpent design in tribute to Quetzalcoatl, showing that in the mind of the Toltecs war and religion went hand in hand.

Chichen Itza rediscovered

The first archaeologists from the outside world to find Chichen Itza were the American travellers John Stephens and Frederick Catherwood. They did not excavate there as they did at Copan, but John Stephens published a description of the ruins in the 1840s.

The next archaeologist on the scene was E. H. Thompson, who discovered the grim secret of the sacred well and its skeletons. But this was not a careful, planned excavation, and Thompson's finds led to some false and exaggerated ideas about life in Chichen Itza.

In 1924 a team of United States archaeologists from the Carnegie Institute began the first planned excavation at Chichen Itza. Their work went on for 17 years and examined the culture of the Toltecs from every point of view. Some of the buildings have been restored to their former glory.

Pueblo Bonito

New Mexico, c. AD 1100–1200

In the pueblos of Chaco Canyon, the Anasazi people lived in huge, fortress-like buildings like modern apartment blocks. Why did they choose to live so close together, and what became of them?

In Chaco Canyon, in the mountains of New Mexico, are the remains of the oldest civilization discovered so far in North America. Chaco Canyon is a strip of land no more than 1 mile (1.6 kilometers) wide and about 12 miles (20 kilometers) long. Nearly 1,000 years ago, when a river flowed through the canyon, it was home to about 10,000 people. They were the Anasazi, the ancestors of the Pueblo people of today.

Living together

Most of the Anasazi lived in stone-built towns called pueblos. The pueblos were quite unlike the cities of any other ancient civilization. They were large, fortress-like buildings on several levels, containing homes for hundreds of people.

A number of these pueblos were built along the Chaco Canyon, linked by a network of roads. The largest of these was Pueblo Bonito, alongside the River Chaco.

Around the outside wall of Pueblo Bonito, the building was four stories high. Inside, there was a lower courtyard area. The people who lived there reached their homes by climbing up ladders on to the roof and then down again into their own rooms.

Built for defense?

Pueblo Bonito was massively built, with thick stone walls inside and out. These may have been for defense, but they would also have helped keep the rooms cool in the fierce desert heat.

Another possible reason for living together in the pueblo was that it used less land than if each family had had its own house. With so many people trying to survive on the narrow strip of fertile land in the canyon, every patch of land where crops

Chaco Canyon was as packed with people as present-day Japan. The pueblo, or village, was the only way to find room for them between the river and the cliffs.

DID YOU KNOW?

The thunder spirit looks down from the sky on Pueblo Bonito as an inhabitant makes an offering. To primitive peoples thunderstorms must have been terrifying, but they brought rain for the crops.

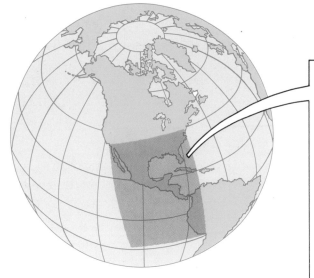

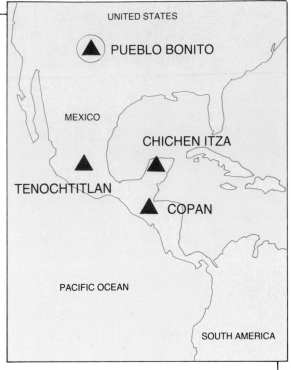

Pueblo Bonito is in northern New Mexico, near the border with Colorado. It is surrounded by the rocky, semi-desert Colorado Plateau. Even today, it is difficult to reach.

could be grown, would be valuable.

The Anasazi had no written language and they left behind no inscriptions and no stone carvings to give us clues to what their lives and culture were like. Our picture has to be pieced together from what the archaeologists found at Pueblo Bonito and the other twelve major sites in the canyon.

Learning by experience

One striking thing is the Anasazi's skill in building, all done with very basic stone tools. They must have had a system of measurement and an understanding of how weight is spread through a building in order to build a complex structure like Pueblo Bonito.

It is possible to see how their skill in building developed over the years. Deep inside Pueblo Bonito there is a core of older rooms built in the same

style but more crudely. Here, the stone is more roughly cut and held together with mud. Handprints on the mud show how it was given a smooth finish by the simplest of methods. The newer houses around the original ones are better finished, and the tools found in them show that the Anasazi had made advances in their technology between the two phases of building.

Their skills extended outside their homes as well. They cut storage pits in the rock for water, which they channeled to the fields along irrigation ditches. Yet, although their ideas seem very modern in some ways, they continued to farm their land using only the most basic tools – digging sticks, stone knives, and stone hoes.

Ladders to the outside world

When the people of Pueblo Bonito

were all inside, with their ladders stored away, they would have been completely safe from attack. We do not know who their enemies were, but possibly there were raiding parties of wandering people, who would have liked to plunder such a prosperous city. Some archaeologists think that this is what happened, but if so, there are no signs of a struggle.

Although Pueblo Bonito looks like a place lived in by people who were afraid of being attacked, the Anasazi did not cut themselves off from the outside world. As well as the road network linking the settlements in Chaco Canyon, they put ladders up the sheer rock faces and cut stone stairways so that they could climb out on to the plateau.

These routes were probably used by traders, but they would also allow the Anasazi to quarry precious stones like turquoise in the mountains. No doubt the meat, such as deer, elk, antelope, and mountain sheep, which the people ate, also arrived in Pueblo Bonito this way.

A peaceful life

Despite the fortress-like appearance of the pueblos, there is nothing to suggest the religious violence or warrior-culture of the Central American civilizations. In fact, the picture that comes to us from the objects that the Anasazi left behind is of a peaceful life. The riverside land around Pueblo Bonito was carefully cultivated to produce maize and perhaps other crops.

Meanwhile, the women stayed at home, spinning, weaving, sewing, and making baskets. Probably, except in the heat of midday, they used the roof of the pueblo as a workshop.

The Kivas

Not all the rooms in Pueblo Bonito were homes. There were also a number of larger underground rooms, known as kivas, which were used for religious ceremonies.

These were all built to a similar pattern, except that some were larger than others. Probably the smaller kivas were used by particular families. All had a stone bench built around the inside wall and a hearth in the centre. When they were found, they were open to the sky, but archaeologists think that they may

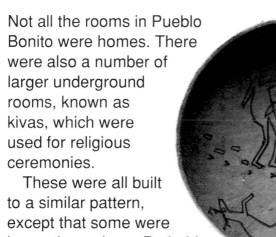

Successful hunters.

have been roofed with logs, with a central hole for smoke from the fire.

What happened in the kivas?

We know very little about the religion of the Anasazi people, so we can only make guesses based on the objects found in the kivas. These include prayer sticks, which could have been used as offerings to the gods, plus torches and pipes. It may be that pipe-smoking had a ceremonial importance, as it did with Native Americans many centuries later.

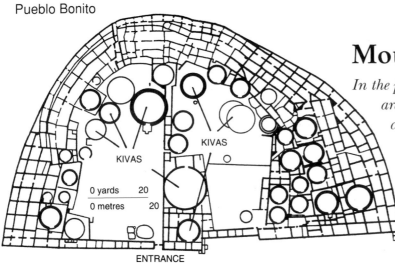

Pueblo Bonito

KIVAS

KIVAS

0 yards 20

0 metres 20

ENTRANCE

Mountain stronghold

In the plan view of Pueblo Bonito, the rectangles are the homes and storerooms and the circles are the kivas. The reconstruction shows how neatly the D-shaped pueblo was fitted into the narrow canyon, with its fields around it, and how safe it was from attack. Enemies would first have to climb down the sheer rock face, and then try to find a way into the building itself. Inside the pueblo, people were free to stroll about or visit each other using the roof as a thoroughfare.

Ideal home

The rocky plateau above Pueblo Bonito, reached by ladders, was a rich source of materials for the Anasazi. They built entirely in stone, except possibly for roofs, and seem to have had little wooden furniture. But they needed timber for ladders and fuel. Turquoise, jet, and copper, which they used in their jewelry, also came from the plateau. So did their meat, as they did not breed animals. With the river beside them and the mountains above them, the Anasazi seem to have found a perfect environment for survival.

Life in Pueblo Bonito

If you think of hundreds of families living in single rooms in a large building with access to the outside only by ladder, it sounds like a cramped way of life. But it may have been less cramped than it seems to us.

Neat and cosy

The living-rooms in the pueblo were quite large – about 13 x 16 feet (4 x 5 meters). The higher rooms had windows, but the lower ones must have been dark and airless and may have been used only for storage.

Near the end of Pueblo Bonito's life some of the lower rooms were used as rubbish dumps – a valuable source of information for archaeologists.

Many of the rooms were linked to a system of ventilation which brought fresh air from outside and carried away smoke from the fires. There are hints that the people of the pueblo went to great efforts to make their lives as comfortable as they could. It seems that they frequently whitewashed the walls of their rooms, for example, to make them lighter and cover up the dirt from the fires.

They seem to have been tidy people. Many of their rooms had poles fixed to the walls to serve as clothes-racks. Some also had built-in shelves or cupboards hollowed out of the stone. They seem to have had little other furniture, but this would have left them more space for living in.

There were stone benches built into the walls of some rooms, but most people in Pueblo Bonito probably sat on the floor for their meals. They probably slept on the floor too, on mats made of rushes or willow shoots, or on blankets.

Because so many people lived in so small an area, it must have been very important to keep everything tidy and put clothes, bedding, and cooking utensils out of danger.

Left: dressed for a religious ceremony.
Below: cutting maize.

Pueblo crafts

Spinning, weaving, pottery, and jewelry-making were among the crafts carried on in Pueblo Bonito, probably by the women.

Around AD 1200, towards the end of the Anasazi civilization, the pottery made at Pueblo Bonito was as good as was being made anywhere else in the world at that time. The potters had developed glazes and paints which enabled them to produce pots decorated with geometrical black-on-white designs.

They had also discovered how to make dyes and paints from different kinds of crushed rock and possibly also from plants. These were used not only on pottery, but also for cloth, and perhaps also as body paint.

Dressing up

The pueblo people were fond of adorning themselves with jewelry. They collected the brightly-colored feathers of such birds as macaws, which they probably used in headdresses. They particularly liked beads, and many thousands have been found in the ruins of Pueblo Bonito.

They liked to make beads out of turquoise (a semi-precious stone), but this was not found locally. Mining parties must have traveled to find it, unless it was obtained from traders.

The jewelry-makers also used jet and copper, but these were also difficult to find, so they turned to materials such as shale, a soft rock found locally. The design of the jewelry was simple, but making it demanded great skill, for example in drilling the minute holes for stringing the beads.

Decorated jug.

Found on maneuvers

Our present knowledge and understanding of Pueblo Bonito is due to the work of Neil M. Judd. He was an American archaeologist who carried out a thorough investigation of Pueblo Bonito in a series of expeditions between the 1930s and the 1950s.

His team experimented with local materials to try to find out how the Anasazi made their pottery and jewelry.

They were impressed with how skilled the Anasazi craftspeople were.

Pueblo Bonito had been discovered nearly 100 years before. Around 1850, an American army officer, Lieutenant James Simpson, was taking part in an expedition against the Navaho people and came across the ruins. He published his account, with a detailed description of what he had seen, in 1852.

Tenochtitlan

Mexico, AD 1415–1520

The Aztecs were such savage people that their neighbors drove them into exile, where they built a new city. But neither its wealth nor the strength of its army could save Tenochtitlan when the Spaniards came.

"Go," the god Huitzilopochtli told the Aztec people, "and travel until you come to a place where an eagle sits on a cactus eating a serpent. When you have found it, build your city there." (Huitzilopochtli is pronounced Whitzil-o-pock-tli.)

The Aztecs wandered for many years, looking for such a place. At last they found it, on an island surrounded by marshland. They called their city Tenochtitlan (pronounced Ten-ok-titlan), meaning "the place of the cactus."

Unpopular arrivals

The Aztecs were a wandering people who, some time around AD 1200, came from the north to settle in Mexico. They found themselves in the midst of a struggle for land between a number of warring tribes.

The Aztecs were so barbaric that these other tribes joined in expelling them from their new home, and by AD 1319

the Aztecs were again wanderers. It was then, Huitzilopochtli told them about the eagle.

At first sight, the place where he had led them was an unlikely spot to build a city. The site of Tenochtitlan was marshland surrounding Lake Texcoco. The water was salty and not fit to drink, and there was no wood or stone for building. But the site had good points, as well.

The land round about was good for farming, and the abundant wildfowl on the marsh promised a steady supply of meat. After their wanderings, the Aztecs were looking for a place of safety, and the marsh offered this also.

The Aztecs began building Tenochtitlan around 1350. They reclaimed land from the marsh by building platforms of mud and water plants, with basketwork barriers around the edges. Then

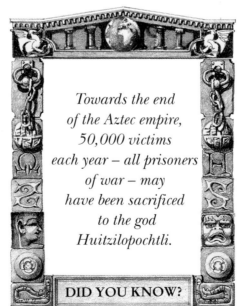

Towards the end of the Aztec empire, 50,000 victims each year – all prisoners of war – may have been sacrificed to the god Huitzilopochtli.

DID YOU KNOW?

The eagle which showed the Aztecs where to built their new city dominates this collection of figures from the legendary history of the Aztec people. In the center background is the great pyramid of Tenochtitlan, with its twin temples.

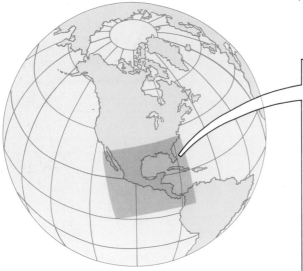

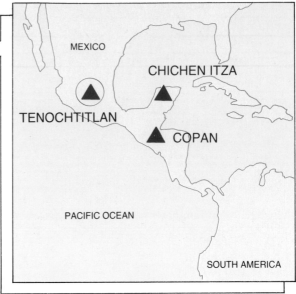

Tenochtitlan is under modern-day Mexico City. After 1520, the waters of Lake Texcoco retreated, leaving a plain.

they planted trees whose roots twined with the basketwork, and this stopped the reclaimed land from being washed away. They used the land for both farming and housing.

At first the Aztecs built wooden houses supported on poles sunk deep in the mud. But their skill at reclaiming land and building on it grew rapidly, and by about 1415 Tenochtitlan was a real city, with its main buildings made of stone from the mountains.

Over the next hundred years it continued to grow, until by 1520 it had a population of about 200,000. By then it had become a truly splendid city. But it was also a city of terror.

Trade and tribute

From the start, the Aztecs of Tenochtitlan had to trade with their neighbors for building materials and other supplies. It was not long before trade turned to war, and by 1400 the Aztecs had a huge empire.

They allowed the conquered peoples to keep their own leaders and worship their own gods, as long as "tribute" – a kind of ransom – of such things as metal, jade, turquoise, and cotton was paid. Tribes which failed to pay their tribute were attacked, and prisoners were taken. What happened to these prisoners is the most bloodthirsty part of the Aztec story.

Hearts for the sun god

In the Aztec religion, Huitzilopochtli was the god of creation and of war. He was represented by the sun. The Aztecs, correctly recognizing that the sun was the source of life on earth, believed that only continuous sacrifices of human hearts and blood would keep them in the sun god's favor.

War provided victims for these sacrifices. Countless thousands of prisoners were brought back from the lands of the Aztec empire. They were taken up the steps to the temple of Huitzilopochtli at the top of the highest pyramid in Tenochtitlan. There, while they were still alive, their hearts were cut out by Aztec priests and their bodies thrown down the steps.

Some archaeologists have estimated that as many as 10,000 victims a year may have met their death in this way. Hundreds of skulls were found stored on shelves near Huitzilopochtli's temple.

A place for everyone

Tenochtitlan was a highly organized society in which everyone had his or her place. At the top was the king, who was so remote from the ordinary people that they were not even allowed to look at him. He had a council of advisers and military commanders who made up the government.

This group, together with the priests, made up the highest class of Aztec society and benefited most from the wealth of the empire. Below these people were judges, officials, merchants, and army officers. Then came the skilled craftsmen, and finally, at the bottom of the ladder, the peasants who worked in the city or in the fields.

The merchants were a particularly powerful group. As they traveled far and wide, they made useful spies and often brought back information for the king about what was happening in the distant corners of his empire. Payment for this information added to the wealth they obtained from their normal trading activities.

The birth of Huitzilopochtli

Aztec legend tells how the sun god, Huitzilopochtli, drove the moon and stars from the sky.

His mother was Coatlicue (pronounced Co-at-li-queue) the earth goddess. She lived with her daughter

Carving of the Aztec earth goddess.

Coyolxauhqui (pronounced Coi-ol-how-kwee), the moon goddess, and the moon goddess's 400 star-god sons.

One day a ball of feathers fell from the sky on to Coatlicue, and she became pregnant. When Coyolxauhqui heard of this, she plotted with her 400 sons to kill her mother. But as the star gods crept up on Coatlicue, Huitzilopochtli sprang from her womb. He was already armed with a blue shield and a spear. On his left leg he wore hummingbird feathers, and on his head he wore a feathered headdress.

Huitzilopochitli first killed Coyolxauhqui with a single blow, and then chased her 400 sons until he had killed them too. And so the sun god, the Aztecs believed, defeated the gods of the night and established his rule over the earth. He became the god of creation and the god of war.

City of canals

Once the Aztecs had mastered the technique of reclaiming land, there was no limit to the number of islands they could build to cope with their growing population. This reconstruction shows what Tenochtitlan looked like round about AD 1475. By then, the city covered an area of almost 4 square miles (1,000 hectares).

Like Venice today, Tenochtitlan was a city of islands connected by waterways. These canals

were crossed by many bridges connecting the streets and alleyways, and three wide raised roads linked the islands with the center. Water transport was used for everyday purposes: people and goods moved about the city by canoe, while rubbish was collected by big barges, which towed it away for dumping.

Many of the homes were built around courtyards where people grew vegetables and

reared turkeys. The windows of most of the houses opened on to the courtyards, giving the occupants protection from flood or attack.

Zoned city
In many ways, Tenochtitlan was organized like a modern city. It was divided into separate areas housing specialist craft workers or traders, or peasants who worked together. These areas were called calpulli. Each calpulli had its own temple and school, where boys were trained for the army. An elder from each calpulli was elected to the city government.

At the heart of the city, where the three wide roads met, was the Sacred Precinct, the area containing Tenochtitlan's main pyramid temples. It was surrounded by a high wall decorated with carved serpents' heads.

The Sacred Precinct

The walled collection of temples at the heart of Tenochtitlan was the center of the Aztec religion. Its pyramids and courtyard temples were dedicated to the Aztec gods. There was also a court for the sacred ball game, a link with the earlier cultures of the Maya and the Toltec.

A carving of Tlaloc.

of Huitzilopochtli, skulls were picked out in white against a red background. Tlaloc's temple was decorated with blue and white stripes.

Excavations have shown that there was a continuous program of rebuilding and restoration to keep the great pyramid and its temples in good repair.

The great pyramid

The Sacred Precinct was dominated by a great pyramid covering an area of about 330 x 260 feet (100 x 80 meters) at its base and standing 100 feet (30 meters) high. Flights of steps led to the top, where there were two temples.

One was to Huitzilopochtli, the god of the sun and of war. It was there that the Aztecs sacrificed prisoners of war. The second temple was to Tlaloc (pronounced T-lal-ok), the same rain god that the Toltec worshiped at Chichen Itza.

The Aztecs used all their skill to decorate the pyramid and its temples. Painted heads of the feathered serpent – another reminder of Toltec culture – lined the central staircase. In the temple

Tributes to the gods

Other Aztec gods were also given temples in the Sacred Precinct. They included the Maya gods Quetzacoatl, the feathered serpent god of the wind and the morning star which we call Venus, and Tezcatlipoca, the god of the night sky (see pages 56–57). Another temple is to Huitzilopochtli's mother, Coatlicue the earth goddess.

Human sacrifice was not the only offering that the Aztecs made to their gods. Archaeologists have found more than 7,000 other objects which were left at the temples in tribute. They include statues, masks, conch shells, pieces of coral, carved serpents, and crocodiles.

A stone knife used for human sacrifices.

Doom foreseen

At the height of its wealth and power, the Aztec empire came to a sudden and terrible end.

The story goes that Moctezuma II, the Aztec king, had seen trouble coming. Some years before, soon after he became king, a comet had appeared in the sky. To Moctezuma, this looked like a rival to the sun, so he called for more sacrifices to give Huitzilopochtli strength to fight off the challenge.

The last years of the Aztec empire were the most bloodthirsty yet as Moctezuma's army swept through the lands they conquered taking fresh prisoners for sacrifice. The grisly ceremonies at the top of the great pyramid in Tenochtitlan were held every day. But it was all in vain.

In March 1519, an army of Spanish soldiers led by General Hernán Cortés landed in Mexico. Their arrival was welcomed by the people on the coast, who hoped that Cortés and his army would defeat the Aztecs and recover the land they had conquered. In fact, the coastal people joined forces with the Spanish to march on Tenochtitlan.

Aztec treachery

At first, Moctezuma seemed to welcome Cortés, but he sent a secret force to attack the Spanish camp on the coast. His soldiers returned with the head of a Spanish officer. Furious, Cortés ordered the entire secret army to be burned alive. Moctezuma's treachery had made enemies of the Spaniards.

Soon afterwards the Aztecs rebelled against the invaders, and Moctezuma was forced to appeal to his people to make peace. The angry crowd stoned him to death. With the Aztecs in revolt, Cortés attacked Tenochtitlan, helped by the Aztecs' local rivals. The end came in August 1521 when Cortés stormed the city, cut off its water supply, and set about levelling the hub of the Aztec empire to the ground.

Under the streets of a city

Forgotten by the Spanish invaders, Mexico City was built on the ruins of Tenochtitlan. The Spanish wrote detailed accounts of the Aztec civilization they had discovered and conquered, but it was not until 1978 that the actual locations of temples and palaces were rediscovered.

Since then, there have been full-scale excavations involving the demolition of part of the modern city. Tenochtitlan has now been recognized as a World Heritage site by the United Nations.

An Aztec from the Codex Mendoza.

Machu Picchu

Peru, c. AD 1440–1570

*When Spanish soldiers conquered the lands of the Incas,
they overlooked Machu Picchu. Isolated on a mountain-top, frozen in time,
the site fills in our knowledge of Inca life.*

High on a mountain ridge in the Andes, the Inca stronghold of Machu Picchu (pronounced Match-oo Pee-shoo), was home, 500 years ago, to about 1,000 people. It was not one of the Incas' most important cities – it was far too remote for that – but it is an important archaeological site today because it was almost undisturbed when it was rediscovered about ninety years ago. Almost all the other cities of the Incas were destroyed by Spanish invaders when they took over 400 years ago.

Machu Picchu is located in an earthquake area.

The mountain climate must have been very hard in winter. On top of all that, land for growing crops was in such short supply that terraces had to be laboriously cut out of the mountain.

However, the site had its good points. Surrounded on three sides by cliffs and mountains, it was a natural fortress. It could only be approached from the south, and here they built a massive wall to defend themselves against attack.

Why there?

We do not know what made the people of Machu Picchu choose such a hard place to settle in. It was separated from the Inca capital, Cuzco, by about 60 miles (100 kilometers) of difficult country. This in itself is surprising because the Incas paid great attention to ease of communication in their empire. In addition,

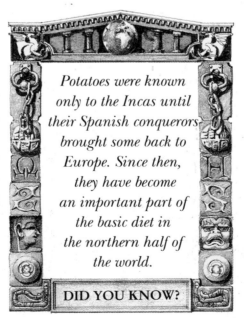

Potatoes were known only to the Incas until their Spanish conquerors brought some back to Europe. Since then, they have become an important part of the basic diet in the northern half of the world.

DID YOU KNOW?

A triumph of building

Another good thing about the site of Machu Picchu was that there was no shortage of stone for building. The people took full advantage of this, and their city was a triumph of the craft of stonemasonry. Not only the houses, but also temples and other ceremonial buildings were all beautifully made of

What is the meaning of the intihuatana, *the sundial cut out of rock in its own temple in Machu Picchu? This picture suggests that it was a sacred stone dedicated to the sun god Inti, and an object of worship.*

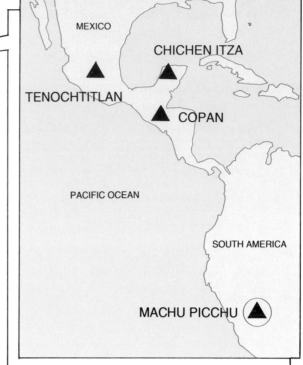

We do not know what the Incas called the city we know as Machu Picchu. Archaeologists named it after the nearest mountain. High up in the Peruvian Andes, it is hidden from the valley below.

blocks of granite cut exactly to fit without using mortar.

On the most important buildings the stones were polished with sand and water and the edges were rounded off, as if to show off the stonemasons' skill. All this was done using only the simplest stone tools.

On the topmost peak of Machu Picchu, the mountain that lent the city its name, the Incas built a tall watchtower which may also have served as a signaling station using smoke signals.

Stairways of rock

The stonemasons of Machu Picchu were equally skilled at cutting shapes out of solid rock. Different levels of the city were linked by flights of steps made in this way. Water channels and storage basins, ponds and fountains were also cut from the rock.

The Incas used their building skills to solve one of the major problems of the Machu Picchu site – the shortage of land for farming. To the south, outside the city wall, the mountain slopes steeply down. Here, the masons built a series of stone walls about 15 feet (5 meters) high. The gaps between these were filled first with gravel and then with topsoil, all transported with great effort from the river valley below. This made fertile terraces on which enough maize and vegetables could be grown to support the population.

Midsummer temple

In the centre of Machu Picchu was a large plaza or square which was probably used as a meeting place. Next to it was a separate, smaller plaza which was Machu Picchu's religious centre.

Here, there were open-fronted stone

shrines and a larger stone temple. One special structure, the intihuatana, looks as if it was positioned so that at dawn on Midsummer Day, the start of the religious year for the Incas, a stone set on an altar caught the first rays of the rising sun.

The son of the sun god

The Incas worshiped many gods, but the sun was the focus of their lives. One of their legends told how Manco Capac, the son of the sun god Inti, taught the Incas to build houses, irrigate the soil, plant crops, and make shoes.

His sister, Mama Ocllo, taught the women how to spin, weave, and sew.

The story went on to explain that Manco Capac founded the Inca capital, Cuzco, and ruled the world from there. The authority of the Incas' emperor came from this legend. Incas believed that their emperor was carrying out Manco Capac's orders, and so they must, in turn, obey him.

This belief that the Inca emperor was ruling in Manco Capac's place gave him enormous power. It also explains why he could easily gather together the large forces of labor necessary to build the empire's road system and the massive walls, stairways, and terraces discovered at Machu Picchu and at many other Inca sites.

The Inca empire

The Incas' own story of how their empire began starts with Manco Capac. Armed with a golden rod, he searched South America for a place where the rod could be pushed deep into the ground and where the soil would therefore be good for crops. He chose the site of Cuzco, where the first Incas settled and which later became the center of their empire.

Cuzco seems to have been founded around AD 1200. It was another 200 years before the Incas, under a new emperor, began to extend their power by conquering neighboring tribes one by one. This process went on until, by 1525, Inca territory stretched along the Andes from Quito, in what is now Ecuador, to the River Maule in Chile, about 2,700 miles (4,300 kilometers) down the coast of South America.

This mountainous empire was not easy to control. The Incas built a network of roads so that troops could be sent to deal quickly with any trouble. The roads – and the bridges woven from climbing plants which were built to cross the rivers – were also used by government officials and by runners who carried messages to and from the capital to outlying parts.

An Inca sacrificial knife.

City in the clouds

Even the most simple houses in Machu Picchu were built to last, with sturdy stone walls. Most had only one story and an open doorway covered with a cloth blind. The roofs were made of thatch, probably of grass found locally.

This reconstruction pictures Machu Picchu as it was around AD 1500. It shows how the builders made use of every available space on the mountainous site. Houses were often built in irregular shapes, narrower at one end than at the other, to fit their plots of land.

Like all aspects of the Incas' lives, their cities were highly organized. In the middle, surrounding the square or plaza, were the temples, other public buildings, and the homes of the most important citizens. In the foreground, near the city wall where the poorer people lived, the houses were smaller and packed more closely together.

Remote from other Inca settlements, the people of Machu Picchu had to be self-sufficient. The terraces on the hillside had to produce enough food to keep them through the winter. Any materials that were not available on the site – such as topsoil for the terraces – had to be painstakingly brought up the mountain from the valley below.

Living in Machu Picchu

Survival in an environment like Machu Picchu meant an endless struggle against all kinds of difficulties. Storms and torrential rains could undo months of careful work in the fields, and the mountain climate played havoc with thatched roofs. In winter it was bitterly cold.

The people used their homes only to eat and sleep in, and they had little furniture except for cupboard spaces cut out of the walls and sometimes a stone bench. Meals were prepared and eaten on the floor, which, covered with matting of reeds or grass, was also used for sleeping.

Early vegetarians

The Incas' diet was almost entirely vegetarian, though they would eat meat if they could get it. Maize – used to make flour and beer – was their basic food. They also grew pumpkins, chilies, beans, potatoes, and coca, a shrub whose leaves were chewed as a drug, though the climate at Machu Picchu would not have suited all of these crops.

Building and farming were the main work for men, and these tasks were tackled with primitive tools. For building, they used stone chisels and scrapers, while the farmers used wooden digging sticks to till the soil and stone machetes for harvesting.

Skill with textiles

While the men were out building or farming, the women would gather together in the open spaces between their homes to spin, weave, dye, and sew. The Incas loved color, and they were good at making dyes out of plants. They also used the dried blood of the insect cochineal, which gave a bright red dye. The yarn they spun was made from the wool of llamas, alpaca and vicuna, which produced very fine, soft material.

The other great Inca craft was pottery, which they made both for everyday and for ceremonial use.

Jar for storing maize beer.

Cutting corn with stone tools.

Counting with string

Although the Incas had no system of writing, they developed a method of counting. This became necessary because of the need to keep a check on the number of men available throughout the empire for army service or for road-building projects.

This was done by teams of traveling officials called *tucricucs* (pronounced two-crik-ooks), who provided a link between the Inca capital, Cuzco, and the territories of the empire. When counting the Inca people, they recorded the results on knotted and colored bundles of strings called *quipus* (pronounced kwee-poohs). Specially trained teams of accountants, or *quipucamayocs* (pronounced kwee-pooh-ka-may-oks), could translate the knots and color codes back into numbers.

We do not know exactly how the Inca system worked, but it was probably similar to the abacus or counting-frame used by the Chinese. It was very efficient. The last Inca emperor was able to gather a room full of gold to ransom himself from the Spanish invaders within days of being told how much they wanted.

The last Inca city?

Machu Picchu was discovered in 1911 by a team of archaeologists led by Hiram Bingham, then professor of Latin American history at Yale University. It was one of the most exciting archaeological finds of all time. The next year, the Yale team carried out a full excavation of the site.

The setting of Machu Picchu on its mountaintop, and the superb condition of the buildings, led Hiram Bingham to believe that he had found the legendary "lost city of the Incas," the center of the Incas' sun worship and the first of their settlements.

The truth was discovered by later archaeologists. Machu Picchu was not the Incas' "lost city." That was Vilcabamba, far away in the Amazon rain forest. The reason Machu Picchu had been so well-preserved was its remote location; the Spanish army, marching through the Inca empire in the late 1520s, had simply failed to find it. But it was far too small and remote to have been a center for religious life.

Although Hiram Bingham's conclusions were wrong, his reputation is still high. After all, it is thanks to his painstaking work at Machu Picchu that we know so much about the daily lives of the Incas. Nowhere else in either South or Central America has a city survived intact.

Storage jar in the shape of a parrot.

Where to go

Although pictures will tell you a lot, it's much better to go to a museum and look at all the things that archaeologists have found from a vanished civilization. You will get an even better idea of how a people lived and worked and what they thought was important by looking at the statues, jewelry, pottery, and other remains.

Some museums have special visiting days when they let you actually touch these ancient things and examine them. Often school visits are allowed special access to items not usually on display, if they are studying a particular period or culture. But **always** check the opening days and times before you try to visit a museum to avoid disappointment.

Museums

The Art Institute of Chicago, Michigan Ave. and Adams St., Chicago, IL 60603, (312) 443-3600.

The Brooklyn Museum, 200 Eastern Pkwy., Brooklyn, NY 11238, (718) 638-5000

The Cleveland Museum of Art, 11150 East Blvd., Cleveland, OH 44106, (216) 421-7340

Dallas Museum of Art, 1717 N. Harwood, Dallas, TX 75201, (214) 922-1200

The Denver Art Museum, 100 W. 14th Ave. Pkwy., Denver, CO 80204, (303) 640-2295

Indianapolis Museum of Art, 1200 W. 38th St., Indianapolis, IN 46208, (317) 923-1331

Los Angeles County Museum of Art, 5905 Wilshire Blvd., Los Angeles, CA 90036, (213) 857-6111

Metropolitan Museum of Art, Fifth Ave. at 82nd St., New York, NY 10028, (212) 879-5500

The Minneapolis Institute of Arts, 2400 Third Ave. S., Minneapolis, MN 55404, (612) 870-3000

Museum of Fine Arts, 465 Huntington Ave., Boston, MA 02115, (617) 267-9300

North Carolina Museum of Art, 2110 Blue Ridge Rd., Raleigh, NC 27607-6494, (919) 833-1935

Philadelphia Museum of Art, 26th St. & Benjamin Franklin Pkwy., Philadelphia, PA 19130, (215) 763-8100

Phoenix Art Museum, 1625 N. Central Ave., Phoenix, AZ 85004-1685, (602) 257-1880

Portland Art Museum, 1219 S.W. Park Ave., Portland, OR 97205, (503) 226-2811

Seattle Art Museum, 100 University St., Seattle, WA 98101, (206) 625-8900

Virginia Museum of Fine Arts, 2800 Grove Ave., Richmond, VA 23221-2466, (804) 367-0844

Specific sites

Catal Hüyük – most of the material from this site is in the Anatolian Civilizations Museum in Ankara, Turkey.

Stonehenge – there is an information center at Stonehenge which explains how the site developed over the centuries. Nearby, the Alexander Keiller Museum at Avebury has displays about the Beaker People, while the Salisbury & South Wiltshire Museum at Salisbury has displays about Stonehenge and the people who built it.

Skara Brae – most of the things found by Professor Childe are in the Royal Museum of Scotland in Edinburgh. The Tankerness House Museum at Kirkwall on Orkney Mainland has a reconstruction of a house from Skara Brae.

Troy – there is a small museum at Troy showing some of the finds from recent excavations. Most of Heinrich Schliemann's finds went to Berlin and disappeared during the Second World War. For the ancient Greeks, the best collection is in the National Archaeological Museum in Athens.

Biskupin – most of the finds from the excavations before 1939 were destroyed during the Second World War. Since 1946 finds from excavations have been housed in a museum at Biskupin.

Copan – there is a small museum in the town near Copan, but the best collection of Mayan material is in the National Archaeological Museum of Mexico in Mexico City.

Chichen Itza – the best collection of Toltec material is in the National Archaeological Museum of Mexico in Mexico City.

Pueblo Bonito – the best collection of material from the Pueblo culture is at the Smithsonian Institution in Washington, D.C.

Tenochtitlan – all the finds from this site are in the Museum of Mexico City in Mexico City.

Machu Picchu – there is a small museum in Cuzco of finds from various Inca sites, but the best collection is in the National Museum of Peru in Lima. There is also a private "Gold Museum" in the suburbs of Lima where gold and silver jewelry and feather garments are on display.

Further Reading

Aratos, Sylvio. *Pueblos*. New York: Facts on File, 1990.

Bannon, John Francis. *History of the Americas*. 2nd ed. New York: McGraw-Hill, 1963.

Bateman, Penny. *Aztecs and Incas*. New York: F. Watts, 1980.

Berdon, Frances. *The Aztecs*. New York: Chelsea House, 1989.

Childress, David Hatcher. *Lost Cities and Ancient Mysteries of South America*. Stelle, IL: Adventures Unlimited Press, 1986.

Clark, Grahame. *Prehistoric Europe*. Stanford: Stanford University Press, 1966.

Edmonds, I. G. *The Mysteries of Troy*. Nashville: T. Nelson, 1977.

Fagan, Brian M. *Ancient North America*. New York: Thames and Hudson, 1991.

Gruzinski, Serge. *The Aztecs*. New York: Abrams, 1992.

Hammond, Norman. *Ancient Maya Civilization*. New Brunswick, NJ: Rutgers University Press, 1982.

Iverson, Peter. *The Navahos*. New York: Chelsea House, 1990.

Karen, Ruth. *Kingdom of the Sun*. New York: Four Winds Press, 1975.

Kendall, Sarita. *The Incas*. New York: New Discovery Books, 1992.

Morrison, Marion. *Atahuallpa and the Incas*. New York: Bookwright Press, 1986.

Snow, Dean R. *The Archaeology of North America*. New York: Viking Press, 1976.

Index